TALK TO ME IN KOREAN

LEVEL 9

Get One Step Closer to Speaking Like a Native
Through Idiomatic Phrases
and More Advanced Grammar Points

This book is based on a series of published lessons, divided into ten levels, which are currently available at TalkToMeInKorean.com.

TALK TO ME IN KOREAN
- LEVEL 9 -

Talk To Me In Korean - Level 9

| 1판 1쇄 | 1st edition published | 2020. 11. 23 |
| 1판 5쇄 | 5th edition published | 2023. 9. 25 |

지은이	Written by	Talk To Me In Korean
책임편집	Edited by	선경화 Kyung-hwa Sun, 김은희 Eunhee Kim, 석다혜 Dahye Seok
디자인	Designed by	선윤아 Yoona Sun
삽화	Illustrations by	김경해 Kyounghae Kim
녹음	Voice Recordings by	선현우 Hyunwoo Sun, 최경은 Kyeong-eun Choi
펴낸곳	Published by	롱테일북스 Longtail Books
펴낸이	Publisher	이수영 Su Young Lee
편집	Copy-edited by	김보경 Florence Kim
주소	Address	04033 서울특별시 마포구 양화로 113. 3층(서교동. 순흥빌딩)
		3rd Floor, 113 Yanghwa-ro, Mapo-gu, Seoul, KOREA
이메일	E-mail	TTMIK@longtailbooks.co.kr
ISBN		979-11-86701-80-5 14710

*이 교재의 내용을 사전 허가 없이 전재하거나 복제할 경우 법적인 제재를 받게 됨을 알려 드립니다.

*잘못된 책은 구입하신 서점이나 본사에서 교환해 드립니다.

*정가는 표지에 표시되어 있습니다.

TTMIK - TALK TO ME IN KOREAN

MESSAGE
FROM
THE AUTHOR

You are amazing. Regardless of how you got here, whether you studied with Talk To Me In Korean all the way from Level 1, or learned Korean elsewhere and found Level 9 suitable for you now, you are amazing. Learning a new language requires an incredible amount of perseverance and dedication, and picking up this book to improve your Korean even more shows that you will go even further.

This book is full of new expressions and grammar points that you can use to speak Korean even more fluently. At the same time it will also work as a reminder that learning and speaking Korean is an integral part of your daily life now. No matter how fluent and comfortable you already are when speaking Korean, your continued effort to improve and learn new things is exciting and commendable.

레벨 9까지 오신 걸 정말 축하드립니다. '나 이제 한국어를 충분히 잘하는데 굳이 더 배울 필요 있나?'라고 생각하지 않고, 이렇게 꾸준히 공부하시는 모습도 정말 멋집니다. 톡투미 인 코리안으로 처음부터 공부하셨든, 아니면 다른 곳에서 한국어를 배웠다가 레벨 9 책을 선택하셨든, 이미 여러분에게 한국어는 생활의 일부분이 되었을 거예요. 앞으로도 꾸준히 공부하시고 계속 실력을 늘리시면, 재미있는 경험과 좋은 기회들이 계속 찾아올 거라고 믿습니다. 계속 응원하겠습니다.

TABLE OF
CONTENTS

LESSON 1

Advanced Idiomatic Expressions 6

손 (Hand)

Track 01

This is an Advanced Idiomatic Expressions lesson related to 손, the hand. In order to fully understand and use the expressions introduced in this series, it is essential that you understand the grammatical structure of the sentences. When you come across a grammar point that you are unfamiliar with, please go back and review the related TTMIK lessons.

Keyword: 손 = hand

I. 손에 익다 = to become accustomed to something

▷ 익다 = to be ripe, to be experienced

You might be familiar with the word 익숙하다, which means "to be used to" something. Here, the verb 익다 has the same meaning as 익숙하다. However, when the word 손 is used, the expression is always used in the form 손에 익다. Think of it as your hand being "comfortable with" or "accustomed to" a task or skill.

8

Ex)

아직 일이 손에 익지 않아서, 시간이 오래 걸려요.

= I have not become accustomed to the work yet, so it takes me a long time.

2. 손을 씻다 = to be through with something (bad); to quit doing something (bad)

The verb 씻다 means "to wash", so the literal meaning of 손을 씻다 is "to wash one's hands". While it can be used in this literal sense, the expression 손을 씻다 can also be used to mean "to quit doing something bad", such as quitting criminal or illegal activity. You will hear this a lot in movies.

Track
01

Ex)

저는 그 일에서 손 씻은 지 오래됐어요.

= It has been a long time since I quit doing that.

3. 손이 크다 = to be openhanded; to be very generous (usually with the food that one cooks)
  ▷ 크다 = to be big

When someone tends to make a lot of food when cooking, you can say that the person is 손이 크다. When this expression is used idiomatically, it has nothing to do with a person's hand size. 손이 크다 is usually, if not always, used to refer to mothers who cook more food than is necessary.

Ex)

저희 어머니는 손이 커서 항상 음식을 너무 많이 하세요.

= My mother is openhanded, so she always cooks too much food.

4. 손에 땀을 쥐다 = to be thrilled (while experiencing or watching something)

▷ 땀 = sweat

▷ 쥐다 = to grab

Literally, 손에 땀을 쥐다 means "to grab sweat in one's hand". The actual meaning of this phrase is that you are so excited and thrilled that your hands start sweating. This expression is commonly used in the forms 손에 땀을 쥐고, meaning "while being very thrilled", and 손에 땀을 쥐게 하는, meaning "to be thrilling".

Note that this is mostly used when talking about something that you enjoy watching or experiencing. On the other hand, if your hands started to sweat because you watched a horror film and you are scared, you would instead say, "손에 땀이 나다 (= one's hands sweat)" instead of using this idiomatic phrase.

Ex)

축구 경기가 너무 재미있어서 정말 손에 땀을 쥐고 봤어요.

= The soccer match was a lot of fun, so it was thrilling to watch. / The soccer match was a lot of fun and I was really on the edge of my seat.

5. 손에 안 잡히다 = cannot concentrate on something (usually one's work)

▷ 잡히다 = to be grabbed, to be caught

When you say that something is 손에 안 잡히다, it literally means that something is "not caught in one's hands". However, the actual meaning is that you cannot get started on a task or cannot concentrate on something because you are distracted by other worries or exciting things.

Ex)

걱정돼서 일이 손에 안 잡혀요.

= I cannot concentrate on work because I am worried.

6. 손을 놓다 = to stop working on something; to release one's hold on something

▷ 놓다 = to let go

When you release or take your hands off of something, you are not working on it anymore. You can say 손을 놓다 when you are distracted or discouraged and are no longer working on something.

Ex)

요즘 비디오 만드는 것에 손을 놓고 있었어요.

= Recently, I have not been making any videos.

외국어 공부하는 것에 손을 놨다가 다시 시작했어요.

= I stopped studying a foreign language for a bit, but started again.

Track
01

7. 손이 닳도록 빌다 = to beg as if one's life depended on it; to beg and plead

▷ 닳다 = to be worn down

▷ 빌다 = to beg, to plead

빌다 is to beg or to plead, and 손이 닳도록 means "to the point where your hands will be worn out", so all together, 손이 닳도록 빌다 means "to plead or beg as if your life depended on it".

Ex)

손이 닳도록 빌었는데도, 안 된다고 했어요.

= I begged and begged, but he still said no.

Another time you can use this is when someone does something really bad. In response, you can say to them, "너는 손이 닳도록 빌어야 돼 (= You have to keep begging for forgiveness until your hands are worn out)."

8. 손을 떼다 = to pull out of something

▷ 떼다 = to detach

떼다 means "to detach something off another thing". So, when you say that you detach your hands from something, it means that you have stopped doing something. While 손을 놓다, 손을 떼다, and 손을 씻다 all have similar meanings, 손을 씻다 usually means "to stop doing something that is bad or illegal", 손을 놓다 means "to be too distracted or tired to continue working on something", and 손을 떼다 means "to decide to stop being involved in something from a certain moment".

Ex)

저는 이 일에서 손 뗄게요.

= I will pull out of this.

= I will stop being involved in this project.

* If you say "저는 이 일에서 손 놓을게요", it means that you will not care about or pay attention to this project anymore. However, if you say "저는 이 일에서 손 뗄게요", it means that you personally will stop being involved in this project, but other people might continue to work on it, and you might continue to have an interest in it although you will not work on it directly.

Sample Dialogue

Track 02

주연: 예지야, 우리 과제 빨리 끝내야 된다니까 왜 손 놓고 있어.

예지: 사실 오늘 아침에 엄마랑 싸워서 지금 아무것도 손에 안 잡혀.

주연: 그랬구나. 그럼 그렇게 걱정만 하지 말고 어머니께 빨리 사과드려.

예지: 응, 집에 가자마자 손이 닳도록 빌어야 될 것 같아.

Jooyeon: Yeji, we have to hurry up and finish our project, why did you stop working?

Yeji: Actually this morning I got into a fight with my mom so I can't concentrate on anything.

Jooyeon: I see. Well, then don't just sit there worrying, hurry up and apologize to your mom.

Yeji: Yeah, as soon as I get home I think I need to beg for forgiveness.

✐ Exercises for Lesson 1

Fill in the blanks with the appropriate idioms with 손 from the lesson.

Check the answers on **p. 216**

1. (   )

   = to stop working on something; to get one's hands off something

2. (   )

   = to be through with something (bad); to quit doing something (bad)

3. (   )

   = to be openhanded; to be very generous (usually with the food that one cooks)

4. (   )

   = to be thrilled (while experiencing or watching something)

5. (   )

   = to become accustomed to something

14

LESSON **2**

Completed Action

-아/어/여 버리다

In this lesson, we are going to take a look at the grammar structure, -아/어/여 버리다. This structure is used to express the completion of a certain action. In addition to an action being completed, this structure also includes the speaker's feeling, which can be (1) a happy feeling about finally completing a task and being unburdened, or (2) a sad feeling that something happened in a way that the speaker did not want or expect.

Track
03

Conjugation

Verb stem + -아/어/여 버리다

Ex)

끝나다 = to finish; to end

→ 끝나 버리다 = to finish; to come to an end

→ 끝나 버렸어요. = It ended (and I am sad about it). / It ended (and it is completely over).

15

The construction is fairly simple, but it might take some time to get used to the actual meaning behind this grammar structure, especially when you want to determine whether the feeling contained in the sentence is a happy one about completing a task or a sad one about something ending.

Examples of a happy feeling attached to -아/어/여 버리다

I. 다 끝내 버렸어요!

＝ I have finished everything!

* You could just say, "다 끝냈어요" but this is a very plain way of saying you finished something. By adding 버리다, you are adding more feeling to the phrase.

Track
03

2. 고민하다가, 사 버렸어요!

＝ I was hesitating, but I (finally) bought it!

* Again, saying, "샀어요" alone does not express a lot of emotion. It is as if you bought something but did not necessarily think hard about it before buying it. However, adding 버리다 adds more feeling to the sentence.

Examples of a sad feeling attached to -아/어/여 버리다

I. 잃어버렸어요.

＝ I lost it (and I am not happy about it).

* Since people almost always add -아/어/여 버리다 to 잃다, 잃어 버리다 has become one word, 잃어버리다.

2. 떨어져 버렸어요.

＝ It dropped (and I did not want it to).

16

Sample Sentences

어제 산 핸드폰을 잃어버렸어요.

= I lost the cell phone I bought yesterday. (And I did not want that to happen.)

    * In this kind of sentence, simply saying, "잃었어요", does not accurately express one's emotion, so we add 버리다 to add more of a feeling of sadness.

안 좋은 일은 다 잊어버렸어요.

= I have forgotten all the bad things. (I am done with them.)

    * 잊어 버리다 has also become one word, 잊어버리다, since people say it this way so often.

    ** You might hear people say, "안 좋은 일은 빨리 잊어버리세요", which means, "Forget all the bad things and be done with it."

빨리 끝내 버리세요.

= Get it over with quickly.

= Finish it quickly and be done with it already.

    * You could say, "빨리 끝내세요", but adding 버리다 expresses your feelings and intent to the listener more clearly.

Track 03

벌써 다 말해 버렸어요.

= I have already told them everything. (It is done. It is over.)

10분 더 기다려도 안 오면 저 혼자 가 버릴 거예요.

= If I wait for 10 more minutes (and) you do not come, I will just go by myself.

    * By using 버리다 in this situation, you are implying that you are angry.

어제 쓴 글이 마음에 안 들어서 다 지워 버렸어요.

= I did not like what I wrote yesterday, so I have erased it all.

17

예지 씨한테 기다려 달라고 했는데, 그냥 가 버렸어요.

= I asked Yeji to wait, but she just left.

컴퓨터가 멈춰 버렸어요.

= My computer has frozen. (And it is causing me trouble.)

시작한 김에 오늘 다 끝내 버리는 거 어때요?

= Now that we have started it, why don't we just get it all done today?

영화가 벌써 시작해 버렸어요.

= Oh, no! The movie has already begun!

    * With this kind of expression, the meaning changes depending on your delivery. You

    can use 버리다 to express that you are either happy or that you are upset.

**Track
03**

18

Sample Dialogue

Track
04

유정: 저 남편이 사 준 목걸이를 잃어버렸어요.

지연: 정말요? 그거 유정 씨가 진짜 아꼈던 목걸이잖아요. 어디에서 잃어버렸어요?

유정: 모르겠어요. 어딘가에 떨어졌는데 제가 그냥 지나쳐 버린 것 같아요.

지연: 사무실에 있을 수도 있어요. 저랑 같이 찾아 봐요.

Yujeong: I lost the necklace my husband bought for me.

Jiyeon: Really? That necklace was really special to you. Where did you lose it?

Yujeong: I don't know. It fell off somewhere and I think I didn't notice.

Jiyeon: It could be in the office. Let's look for it together.

Check the answers on **p. 216**

✏ Exercises for Lesson **2**

Rewrite the following using **-아/어/여 버리다** *to express either a happy feeling about finally completing a task and getting rid of a burden, or a sad feeling about something happening in a way that the speaker did not want or expect.*

Ex) 끝났어요. = It ended.

→ <u>끝나 버렸어요</u>. = It ended (and I am sad about it). / It ended (and it is completely over).

I. 샀어요. = I've bought it.

→ .... = I have (finally) bought it.

2. 떨어졌어요. = It dropped.

→ .... = It dropped (and I did not want it to).

3. 벌써 다 말했어요. = I have already told them everything.

→ .... = I have already told them everything. (It is done. It is over.)

4. 컴퓨터가 멈췄어요. = My computer has frozen.

→ .... = My computer has frozen. (And it is causing me trouble.)

5. 영화가 벌써 시작했어요. = The movie has already begun.

→ .... = Oh, no! The movie has already begun!

LESSON **3**

Advanced Situational Expressions 7

기분 나쁠 때
(When You Are Unhappy)

Track 05

Welcome to another lesson in the Advanced Situational Expressions series. Throughout this series, we go over common situations and some of the advanced Korean expressions you can use in each of them. In this lesson, we will introduce various expressions you can use when you are unhappy about something or are upset about a particular situation.

1.

오늘 기분이 너무 안 좋아요.

= I am feeling terrible today.

= I am so upset today.

2.

지금 그럴 기분 아니에요.

= I am not in the mood for that.

* You might use this if you are not in a good mood and someone teases you a bit.

21

3.

지금 이야기할 기분 아니에요. 말 시키지 마세요.

= I am not in the mood to talk now. Please leave me alone.

* "말 시키지 마세요" literally means "Do not make me talk." By saying this, you may seem like an unfriendly person.

4.

진짜 열 받는 일이 있었어요.

= Something really maddening happened.

= I am so mad right now because of something that happened earlier.

* 열 means "heat", so people use the expression 열 받다 when they are angry and can feel the heat from their anger and their blood is boiling.

Track 05

5.

사람이 어떻게 그래요?

= How can someone be so mean?

= How could they do that to me?

6.

진짜 어이가 없네.

= I do not even know what to say. I am so mad.

* You can say this to yourself when you are at a loss for words.

7.

저 지금 너무 화나는데 참고 있는 거예요.

= I am so mad right now, but I am trying not to show it.

8.

진짜 속상해요.

= I am so upset.

= I am so sad.

* 속 = inner part / 상하다 = to rot

9.

너무 서운해요.

= I am so disappointed.

10.

이번에는 믿고 있었는데 완전 실망했어요.

= I trusted them this time, but I am really disappointed.

* 완전 is originally a noun but in spoken Korean, it is often used colloquially as an adverb to mean "totally" or "really".

Track
05

23

Sample Dialogue

Track 06

우현: 진짜 어이가 없네.

진혁: 왜요? 무슨 일 있었어요?

우현: 제 돈 빌려 간 친구가 제 전화를 계속
안 받았거든요. 근데 여기 보세요.
이렇게 여행 가서 사진 올렸어요.

진혁: 진짜요? 와, 사람이 어떻게 그래요?

Woohyeon: I seriously can't believe this.

Jinhyuk: Why? What happened?

*Woohyeon: My friend who borrowed money from
me won't pick up the phone when I call.
But look at this. He went on vacation and
uploaded pictures.*

Jinhyuk: Really? Wow, how could he be like that?

✎ Exercises for Lesson 3

1. When you are not in the mood to talk, what can you say in Korean?

① 지금 이야기할 기분 아니에요.

② 사람이 어떻게 그래요?

③ 이번에는 믿고 있었는데 완전 실망했어요.

④ 저 지금 너무 화나는데 참고 있는 거예요.

2. What can you say when you are at a loss for words?

① 진짜 속상해요.

② 오늘 기분이 너무 안 좋아요.

③ 진짜 어이가 없네.

④ 너무 서운해요.

3. When you are about to talk about something maddening that happened earlier, what can you start off by saying?

① 저 지금 너무 화나는데 참고 있는 거예요.

② 진짜 열 받는 일이 있었어요.

③ 말 시키지 마세요.

④ 지금 그럴 기분 아니에요.

Check the answers on **p. 216**

✐ Exercises for Lesson 3

4. Choose the one that is NOT what you can say to someone you are mad at.

① 너무 서운해요.

② 이번에는 믿고 있었는데 완전 실망했어요.

③ 사람이 어떻게 그래요?

④ 진짜 열 받는 일이 있었어요.

5. Choose the one that can only be used in response to someone.

① 진짜 열 받는 일이 있었어요.

② 오늘 기분이 너무 안 좋아요.

③ 지금 그럴 기분 아니에요.

④ 진짜 속상해요.

Check the answers on **p. 216**

LESSON 4

Completed Action

-고 말다

In this lesson, we are going to look at the sentence ending -고 말다. First of all, please note that this sentence ending is more commonly found in written Korean than in spoken Korean. -고 말다 is used to express how a certain action comes to an end or is completed after going through a series of events. It is similar to the sentence ending -아/어/여 버리다, but -고 말다 tends to be more objective. On the other hand, -아/어/여 버리다 tends to show the speaker's feelings about the situation more clearly, and is also used more often in spoken Korean.

Track 07

> ### *Conjugation*
> Verb stem + -고 말다

When you talk about an action in a simple statement and do not provide a lot of background information, using -고 말다 can be inappropriate. For example, if you want to start a conversation by saying "저 어제 이거 샀어요 (= I bought this yesterday)", saying "저 어제 이거 사고 말았어요" instead is awkward. This is because when you use -고 말다 you are expecting the listener to already have an understanding of what kind of situation or previous actions you went through before reaching that final stage of purchasing.

27

Examples

1.

잠들다 = to fall asleep

잠들었어요. = I fell asleep.

잠들고 말았어요. = (I was doing something else, so I did not want to fall asleep, but after a while, eventually) I fell asleep.

* It is more natural to include additional information other than, "잠들고 말았어요", so you would want to add what you were doing before you fell asleep.

공부를 하다가 잠들고 말았어요. = I was studying, but then I fell asleep.

2.

Track 07

감기에 걸리다 = to catch a cold

감기에 걸렸어요. = I caught a cold.

감기에 걸리고 말았어요. = I ended up catching a cold.

As you can see in both of the examples above, the result is somewhat undesirable. However, the result is not always undesirable, and there is usually less of a negative feeling from the speaker about the situation when using -고 말다 than when using -아/어/여 버리다.

Sample Sentences

결국 힘이 다 빠지고 말았어요.

= I ended up using all my energy and was exhausted.

(Meaning: You tried your best to continue, but eventually, after a series of actions, you became exhausted.)

이곳도 사막이 되고 말았어요.

= This place has also become a desert.

(Meaning: The place was not a desert before, but after going through a series of events, it has eventually become a desert, much to your disappointment.)

너무 어두워서 머리를 벽에 부딪히고 말았어요.

= It was too dark, so I ended up hitting my head against the wall.

(Meaning: You were trying not to get hurt and did your best to find your way around even though the room was dark, but eventually, you hit your head against the wall.)

범인을 쫓아갔지만 놓치고 말았어요.

= I chased after the criminal, but I lost him.

(Meaning: You made an effort to go after the criminal and catch him, but eventually, you lost him.)

가겠다는 약속을 하고 말았어요.

= I ended up promising to go.

(Meaning: You did not want to go, or were not supposed to go, but you ended up promising someone that you would go somewhere, perhaps after talking with them.)

Sample Dialogue

캐시: 저 유튜브 시작했는데 악플이 조금씩
　　　달리고 있어요.

새라: 진짜요? 그런 댓글은 읽지 마세요.

캐시: 저도 안 읽으려고 했는데, 읽고 말았어요.

새라: 안 보는 게 좋아요. 안 그러면 금방
　　　그만두고 말 거예요.

*Cassie: I started a YouTube channel but people
started to leave mean comments.*

*Sarah: Really? Don't read those kinds of
comments.*

*Cassie: I wasn't going to read them, but I wound
up reading them anyway.*

*Sarah: It's better not to look at them. Otherwise,
you'll end up quitting right away.*

✏ *Exercises for Lesson* **4**

Check the answers on **p. 216**

Rewrite the following sentences using **-고 말다** *so that they can express how a certain action comes to an end or is completed after going through a series of events.*

> **Ex)** 잠들었어요. = I fell asleep.
>
> → 잠들고 말았어요. = (I was doing other things, so I did not want to fall asleep, but after a while, eventually) I fell asleep.

I. 감기에 걸렸어요. = I caught a cold.

→ .... = I ended up catching a cold.

2. 이곳도 사막이 되었어요. = This place has also become a desert.

→ .... = This place has also ended up becoming a desert.

3. 너무 어두워서 머리를 벽에 부딪혔어요. = It was too dark, so I hit my head against the wall.

→ .... = It was too dark, so I ended up hitting my head against the wall.

4. 범인을 쫓아갔지만 놓쳤어요. = I chased after the criminal, but I lost him.

→ .... = I chased after the criminal, but I ended up losing him.

5. 가겠다는 약속을 했어요. = I promised to go.

→ .... = I ended up promising to go.

31

LESSON 5

Advanced Situational Expressions 8

걱정될 때
(When You Are Worried)

Track 09

Welcome to another lesson in the Advanced Situational Expressions series. Throughout this series, we take a look at common situations and some of the advanced expressions you can use in each of them. In this lesson, we will introduce various expressions you can use when you are worried about something or worried about a particular situation.

1.

걱정돼요.

= I am worried.

= It worries me.

2.

불안해요.

= I am anxious.

= I feel nervous.

* "걱정돼요" is stronger than "불안해요". Typically, you are usually "불안해요" at first, and then if the problem is not resolved and you become even more worried, you become "걱정돼요."

3.

걱정돼 죽겠어요.

= I am worried to death.

= I am so worried.

4.

불안해 미치겠어요.

= I am so anxious (that) it is driving me crazy.

5.

-(으)ㄹ까 봐 걱정이에요.

= I am worried that ... might happen.

= I am worried that they might...

Track 09

Ex)

다칠까 봐 걱정이에요. = I am worried you might get hurt.

늦을까 봐 걱정이에요. = I am worried I will be late.

너무 어려울까 봐 걱정이에요. = I am worried it might be too difficult.

너무 쉬울까 봐 걱정이에요. = I am worried it might be too easy.

경은 씨가 화낼까 봐 걱정이에요. = I am worried that Kyeong-eun might get angry.

6.

-(으)면 어떡하죠?

= What if ... happens?

= What if they...?

Ex)

화내면 어떡하죠? = What if she gets angry at me?

경화 씨가 늦으면 어떡하죠? = What if Kyung-hwa is late?

7.

어떻게 하면 좋죠?

= What should we do?

* This sentence can also be shortened to "어떡하면 좋죠?"

8.

마음이 안 놓여요.

= I feel uneasy.

= I cannot stop worrying.

* 놓이다 is the passive voice of 놓다.

9.

Track 09

잘 해결됐으면 좋겠어요.

= I hope the problem is resolved well.

10.

큰일이네요.

= That is not good.

= That is a big problem.

11.

이 상황에서 어떻게 걱정이 안 돼요?

= How can you not worry in this situation?

34

Sample Dialogue

Track
10

경화: 불안해 미치겠어요. 오늘 대학원
합격자 발표 날이거든요.

석진: 걱정하지 마세요. 합격할 거예요.

경화: 아니에요. 너무 불안해요. 불합격하면
어떡하죠?

석진: 그럴 리가 없어요. 열심히 했으니까
붙을 거예요.

*Kyung-hwa: I'm so anxious, it's making me crazy.
Today is the day they announce grad
school acceptances.*

Seokjin: Don't worry. You'll get in.

*Kyung-hwa: No. I'm too nervous. What if I don't
get in?*

*Seokjin: There's no way. You worked really hard, so
you'll get in.*

✎ Exercises for Lesson 5

Translate each sentence into Korean using the expressions from the lesson on the lines provided.

1. I am anxious.

....

2. What if Kyung-hwa is late?

....

3. I hope the problem is resolved well.

....

Check the answers on **p. 216**

4. I feel uneasy.

....

5. I am worried to death.

....

LESSON **6**

Advanced Idiomatic Expressions 7

발 (Foot)

This is an Advanced Idiomatic Expressions lesson related to 발, the foot. In order to fully understand and use the expressions introduced in this series, it is essential that you understand the grammatical structure of the sentences. When you come across a grammar point that you are unfamiliar with, please go back and review the related TTMIK lessons.

Track
11

Keyword: 발 = foot

1. 발이 넓다 = to be well-connected

　▷ 넓다 = to be wide

You can use this expression to describe how someone has a strong social network and knows many people in various fields. In this expression, 발 symbolizes the scope of one's reach or influence. If you want to literally describe someone's feet as being large or wide, you would say 발이 크다.

37

Ex)

그 사람은 발이 진짜 넓은 것 같아요. 모르는 사람이 없어요.

= He seems like he is really well-connected. There is not one person he does not know.

2. 발 벗고 나서다 = to throw oneself into a matter with enthusiasm

▷ 벗다 = to take off

▷ 나서다 = to come forward

When someone you know is in trouble, or when you see a problem, even if it is not directly related to you, sometimes you want to help. In that case, you can say 발 벗고 나서다 to describe how you enthusiastically throw yourself into the situation. Here, 발 벗다 means "to take off your shoes to go into a room to do something", but it is only used as an idiomatic expression and is never used literally. If you want to say "to take off (one's) shoes", you would say 신발(을) 벗다.

Ex)

많은 사람들이 우리를 돕기 위해서 발 벗고 나서 줬어요.

= A lot of people went out of their way to help us.

3. 발을 담그다 = to be involved in something

▷ 담그다 = to dip, to soak

When you dip your feet into the water (in a swimming pool or the ocean), you can say 발을 물에 담그다. When you take water (물) out of this phrase and just say 발을 담그다, it means "to get involved in a matter". This expression is usually used to describe how hard it is to quit something once you start.

38

Ex)

드라마 보는 것에 한번 발을 담그면 빠져나올 수 없어요.

= Once you start watching TV dramas, it is not easy to quit (watching them).

4. 발 디딜 틈이 없다 = to be really packed
▷ 틈 = gap

발을 디디다 means "to step on something", usually in order to start walking or to stand on something. You can use the expression **발 디딜 틈이 없다** when you want to describe how a place is really crowded and there is no space for you to move around.

Ex)

요즘 홍대는 밤에 가면 사람이 너무 많아서 발 디딜 틈이 없어요.

= These days, if you go to Hongdae at night, there are so many people (that you can barely find a place to stand).

Track 11

5. 한발 늦다 = to fall a step behind
▷ 늦다 = to be late

This expression is similar to the English expression "to fall a step behind". 한 is the native Korean number for "one", so 한 발 can mean "one foot". However, in this context, it means "one step", and therefore the expression means you are "late by just one step". This is usually used when you just missed a bus or the subway, but not when you are talking about being late for a meeting or for work. You can also use it if you have an idea but someone else came up with it or did it first. When 한 발 is used figuratively in this type of idiomatic expression, it is written without a space.

Ex)

지하철 문이 닫히기 전에 타려고 뛰었는데 한발 늦었어요.

= I ran to get on the train before the doors closed, but I was one step too late.

6. 발 빠르게 움직이다 = to move fast, to do the necessary actions quickly
▷ 빠르게 = quickly
▷ 움직이다 = to move

발 빠르게 움직이다 can mean "to literally and physically move fast". It can also mean "to quickly take care of a problem" or "to quickly do the necessary actions to solve a problem or prevent it from occurring".

Track 11

Ex)

경화 씨가 발 빠르게 움직인 덕분에 문제가 더 커지지 않았어요.

= Thanks to Kyung-hwa, who moved fast, the problem did not escalate.

7. 발이 묶이다 = to be detained, confined, shackled
▷ 묶다 = to tie
▷ 묶이다 = to be tied up

If your feet are tied up by a rope or a chain, you cannot go anywhere. Therefore, when you cannot go anywhere, either because of the situation you are in or because of the weather, you can use the expression 발이 묶이다. 발 here literally means "feet", but it also symbolizes the inability to go somewhere. People often use this expression when there is a lot of rain or snow so they cannot go anywhere or leave the house.

40

Ex)

이곳에 눈이 너무 많이 와서 발이 묶였어요.

= It snowed too much here, so I am stuck inside.

8. 발로 뛰다 = to work hard in the field

▷ 뛰다 = to run

Almost everyone uses their feet to run. It is rare to find someone who runs with their hands, but if you say 발로 뛰다 instead of just 뛰다, it means "to work hard in the field". Therefore, 발로 뛰다 means to actually go out and get first-hand experience, rather than just doing desk work or researching through books.

Track
11

Ex)

컴퓨터 앞에만 앉아 있는 것보다 나가서 직접 발로 뛰면 더 좋은 정보를 얻을 수 있을 거예요.

= Rather than sitting in front of a computer, if you go out and work in the field yourself, you will get better information.

9. 새 발의 피 = a drop in the bucket

▷ 새 = bird

▷ 피 = blood

Except for some large species like the ostrich, birds are usually considered small in comparison to many other animals. If a bird is injured and bleeds from its foot, the amount of blood is usually small because its feet are very small. If you say 새 발의 피, it has a similar meaning to the English phrase "a drop in the bucket". In other words, it means that the

41

situation is insignificant or pales in comparison to something that happened before.

Ex)

이번 일에 비하면 지난번 일은 정말 새 발의 피예요.

= This is nothing compared to what happened last time.

10. **발을 끊다** = to stop visiting

▷ 끊다 = to cut

If there is a place that you visited regularly or often that you have stopped visiting, you can use 발을 끊다 to refer to the fact that you do not go there anymore. 발 here does not mean "feet", but refers to the visit itself. If you cut off the 발 (visit), it means you no longer visit or go to a particular place.

Ex)

살이 많이 쪄서 살을 빼려고 자주 가던 치킨집에 발을 끊었어요.

= I have gained a lot of weight, so in order to lose it I quit going to a chicken restaurant that I used to go to frequently.

Sample Dialogue

Track
12

석진: 아! 한발 늦었네요. 벌써 식당이 꽉 찼어요.

경은: 와! 이 식당은 진짜 인기가 많은가 봐요. 발 디딜 틈이 없네요.

석진: 저 건너편 집으로 갈까요?

경은: 아, 저기는 바뀐 주인이 마음에 안 들어서 발 끊었어요.

Seokjin: Ah! We're one step behind. The restaurant is already packed.

Kyeong-eun: Wow! I guess this restaurant is really popular. There's barely room to move.

Seokjin: Should we go to the place across the road?

Kyeong-eun: Ah, I don't like the new owner of that place so I stopped going there.

✏ Exercises for Lesson **6**

Fill in the blanks with the appropriate idioms with **발** *from this lesson.*

1. (   )

   = to stop visiting

2. (   )

   = to be really packed

3. (   )

   = to fall a step behind

4. (   )

   = to be well-connected

5. (   )

   = to throw oneself into a matter with enthusiasm

Check the answers on **p. 216**

LESSON **7**

Word Builder 18

비(非)

Word Builder lessons are designed to help you understand how to expand your vocabulary by learning and understanding some common and basic building blocks of Korean words. The words and letters introduced through Word Builder lessons are not necessarily all Chinese characters, or 한자, although many of them are, and their meanings can differ from modern-day Chinese. Your goal, through these lessons, is to understand how Korean words are formed and remember keywords to expand your Korean vocabulary from there. You certainly do not have to memorize the Hanja characters in order to do this, but if you want to, feel free!

Today's key word element is 비.

The Chinese character for this is 非. There are many other Chinese characters (or Hanja letters) that are used for 비, so keep in mind that not all words that contain 비 have related meanings.

Track
13

45

The word 비 (非) is related to "not".

비 (not) + 공식 (official) = 비공식 非公式 = unofficial, informal

Ex)
비공식 행사 非公式 行事 = informal event

비 (not) + 회 (gathering) + 원 (member) = 비회원 非會員 = non-member
* If you have a hobby, you can become a 회원 of a club with like-minded people.

Ex)
비회원 출입 금지 非會員 出入 禁止 = Non-members are not allowed. / Members only.
비회원은 글을 못 씁니다. = Non-members may not post here.
비회원입니다. = You are not a member. / You are not signed up.

Track 13

비 (not) + 정 (right) + 상 (always) = 비정상 非正常 = not normal, abnormal, unusual

비 (not) + 주 (master, head) + 류 (flow, stream) = 비주류 非主流 = non-mainstream, fringe group

Ex)
비주류 장르 非主流 -- = non-mainstream genre

비 (not) + 인간 (human) + 적 (of) = 비인간적 非人間的 = inhuman

비 (not) + 범 (ordinary) + 하다 = 비범하다 非凡-- = to be extraordinary

비 (not) + 인 (people) + 기 (energy) = 비인기 非人氣 = unpopular

46

Ex)

비인기 종목 非人氣 種目 = unpopular sports

비인기 주식 非人氣 株式 = unpopular stocks

비 (not) + 공 (official) + 개 (open) = 비공개 非公開 = closed, private

Ex)

비공개 결혼식 非公開 結婚式 = private wedding ceremony

비공개 포스트 非公開 --- = private post

비 (not) + 협 (harmony) + 조 (associate) + 적 (of) = 비협조적 非協調的 = uncooperative

Ex)

왜 이렇게 비협조적이에요? = Why are you so uncooperative?

Track 13

비 (not) + 전 (exclusive) + 문 (door) + 적 (of) = 비전문적 非專門的 = unprofessional

비 (not) + 상 (always) + 구 (door) = 비상구 非常口 = emergency exit

비 (not) + 상 (always) + 계단 (stairs) = 비상계단 非常階段 = emergency staircase

비 (not) + 무장 (armed) + 지대 (zone) = 비무장 지대 非武裝 地帶 = DMZ, demilitarized zone

* A lot of people in Korea just say "DMZ" in English rather than saying the full Korean phrase.

시 (true) + 비 (not) = 시비 是非 = right or wrong

Ex)

시비를 걸다 = to pick a fight

시비를 가리다 = to determine who is right and who is wrong

47

Sample Dialogue

Track
14

캐시: 한국 여자 컬링 팀 올림픽에서 금메달 땄죠?

경화: 아니요, 은메달 땄어요. 그래도 비범한 팀이죠. 컬링은 한국에서 비인기 종목인 데다가 비주류 종목이었거든요.

캐시: 우와, 대단하네요!

Cassie: The Korean women's curling team won the gold medal, right?

Kyung-hwa: No. They got the silver medal. Even so, they're a remarkable team. In Korea, curling was not popular and used to be a fringe event.

Cassie: Wow! That's amazing!

✏️ Exercises for Lesson **7**

1. In Level 4 Lesson 13, we learned that the word element 불(不) means "not" in English. In this lesson, we learned another word element that is related to "not". What is it?

(   )

Fill in the blanks with the appropriate Sino-Korean word from the lesson.

Check the answers on **p. 216**

2. (   ) = unofficial, informal

3. (   ) = emergency exit

4. (   ) = non-member

5. (   ) = closed, private

LESSON 8

Advanced Situational Expressions 9

> # 부탁할 때 (When You Ask For A Favor)

Track
15

Welcome to another lesson in the Advanced Situational Expressions series. Throughout this series, we take a look at common situations and some of the advanced expressions you can use in each of them. In this lesson, we will introduce various expressions you can use when you are asking for a favor or asking someone to do something for you.

1.

부탁이 하나 있어요.

= I have a favor to ask.

* 부탁 = favor

** You can also drop 하나 and just say 부탁이 있어요.

2.

부탁할 게 있는데요.

= I have a favor to ask.

3.

부탁 하나만 할게요.

= Let me ask you a favor.

* Some people also say "부탁 하나만 하자" between friends.

4.

제 부탁 하나만 들어줄 수 있어요?

= Can you do me a favor?

* 부탁(을) 들어주다 = to do someone a favor

5.

어려운 부탁인 건 알지만, 저도 같이 가면 안 될까요?

= I understand if it might be a bit difficult, but could I possibly go with you?

* You can start by saying 어려운 부탁인 건 알지만 in order to sound more polite when you ask someone for a favor. Therefore, this phrase is used a lot when asking someone older than you or when you ask for a big favor.

Track 15

6.

죄송한데요, 혹시 전화기 좀 빌릴 수 있을까요?

= I am sorry, but could I borrow your phone?

* 죄송한데요 = I am sorry, but

** 혹시 = by any chance

7.

저 잠깐만 도와주실 수 있나요?

= Can you help me for just a second?

* In this sentence, using 잠깐만 makes it difficult for the listener to say no. So even though you may need help for longer than just a second you can say this to make it harder for the listener to decline.

51

8.

제발 부탁이니까 오늘은 늦지 마세요.

= I am asking you to please not be late today.

* This is more of a warning or a demand rather than a favor.

** 제발 부탁이니까 will make the listener feel bad.

9.

돌아오는 길에 우유 좀 사다 줄 수 있어요?

= Could you get me some milk on your way back?

10.

편의점에 가는 김에 물 좀 사다 줄 수 있어요?

= Since you are going to the convenience store anyway, can you get me some water?

Track 15

11.

어제 제가 부탁한 거 잊지 마세요.

= Please do not forget what I asked you to do yesterday.

Sample Dialogue

Track
16

경은: 현우 씨, 부탁할 게 있는데요. 혹시
전등 좀 갈아 끼워 줄 수 있을까요?

현우: 그럼요. 전등 어디 있어요?

경은: 지금 나가서 사 오려고요.

현우: 아, 그럼 돌아오는 길에 우유 좀
사다 줄 수 있어요?

경은: 네, 그럴게요.

*Kyeong-eun: Hyunwoo, I have a favor to ask.
Could you possibly change the lightbulb,
please?*

Hyunwoo: Sure. Where is the lightbulb?

Kyeong-eun: I'm going to go out and buy one now.

*Hyunwoo: Ah, in that case, could you buy some
milk on your way back?*

Kyeong-eun: Sure, I'll do that.

Check the answers on **p. 216**

✏ Exercises for Lesson **8**

Translate each sentence into Korean using the expressions from the lesson and write it on the lines provided.

1. I am sorry, but could I borrow your phone?

....

2. Can you help me for just a second?

....

3. Since you are going to the convenience store anyway, can you get me some water?

....

4. Could you get me some milk on your way back?

....

5. Please do not forget what I asked you to do yesterday.

....

LESSON 9

Simplifying A Sentence Ending

-(으)ㅁ

In this lesson, we are introducing a new verb ending which can be used, mainly, in three different ways. -(으)ㅁ is commonly used in everyday Korean in both formal and informal settings, and you can use it to simplify the structure of a sentence that would otherwise be a bit more complicated.

Track
17

-(으)ㅁ changes a verb into a noun form. When the verb stem ends with a vowel, you just add -ㅁ, and when it ends with a consonant, you add -음 at the end. Let us look at the different usages and how -(으)ㅁ is different from other verb endings that make noun forms.

Usages of -(으)ㅁ

I.

By attaching -(으)ㅁ after a verb stem, you can transform the verb into a noun. Basically any verb can be made into a noun in this manner, but there are certain words that are used so commonly with -(으)ㅁ that they are also often used as stand-alone nouns. The following are

55

some of the most common examples:

웃다 (to laugh) – 웃음 (laughter, smile)

울다 (to cry) – 울음 (crying, weeping)

믿다 (to believe, to trust) – 믿음 (belief, trust)
> **Ex)**
> 믿음을 가지세요. = Have some faith.

알다 (to know) – 앎 (knowing, knowledge) [암:]

살다 (to live) – 삶 (life) [삼:]

Track 17

얼다 (to freeze) – 얼음* (ice)
* This does not mean "to be frozen", but refers to frozen water or ice.

졸다 (to doze) – 졸음 (sleepiness, drowsiness)
> **Ex)**
> 졸음 방지 껌 = anti-drowsiness gum
> 경은 씨는 졸음이 올 때 어떻게 해요? = What do you do when you get sleepy, Kyeong-eun?

슬프다 (to be sad) – 슬픔 (sadness)

기쁘다 (to be happy) – 기쁨 (pleasure, joy)

아프다 (to be painful, to be sick) – 아픔 (pain, agony)

젊다 (to be young) — 젊음 (youth)

꾸다 (to dream (a dream)) — 꿈 (dream)

지다 (to carry (luggage) on one's back) — 짐 (luggage)

추다 (to dance) — 춤 (dance)

자다 (to sleep) — 잠 (sleep)

Some of these verbs, such as 추다, 지다, and 꾸다 always have to be used together with their noun forms, whereas other verbs like 자다 and 살다 can be used with or without their noun forms.

Track
17

자다 and 살다 can be used on their own or together with their noun forms, like "잠을 자다 (to sleep)" and "삶을 살다 (to live a life)". One of the reasons one might use the noun form is to modify the noun with other adjectives.

추다, 지다, and 꾸다 can NOT be used on their own, because the meaning will not be clear enough. You always need to use them as a pair with their noun forms, such as "춤을 추다 (to dance)", "짐을 지다 (to carry luggage on one's back)", and "꿈을 꾸다 (to have a dream)".

> **Ex)**
> I want to dance.
> = 춤을 추고 싶어요. (O)
>   추고 싶어요. (X)

2.

-(으)ㅁ can be used to make a sentence or clause into a noun group, so that you can then use the noun group as the object or the subject of a larger sentence structure.

Then, what is the difference between -다는/라는 것 and -(으)ㅁ?

Ex)
Nobody knew that today was my birthday.
= 오늘이 제 생일이라는 것을 아무도 몰랐어요.
= 오늘이 제 생일임을 아무도 몰랐어요.

In the sentence above, "오늘이 제 생일이에요" has been changed to the noun group, "오늘이 제 생일임" and is now the object of the verb 모르다, meaning that nobody knew "오늘이 제 생일임" or "the fact that today is my birthday".

Track 17

In most casual conversations, you should use -다는 것 or -라는 것 instead of -(으)ㅁ. -(으)ㅁ sounds much more formal than -다는 것 or -라는 것, therefore -(으)ㅁ is used more in official documents or more formal situations.

Ex)
He is a Korean person.
= 그 사람은 한국 사람이에요.

I knew that he was Korean.
= 그 사람이 한국 사람이라는 것을 저는 알고 있었어요.
= 그 사람이 한국 사람임을 저는 알고 있었어요.

* The sentence with -이라는 것을 is more likely to be used in everyday colloquial speech. However, in written materials, such as in novels, news articles, official statements, etc., you

will more often see -임을.

** Please note that the marker -은 in 그 사람은 was changed to -이 in the longer sentences. In compound sentences like these, the marker -은/는 often changes to -이/가 when the shorter sentence becomes part of a bigger structure.

Wait, there is another form for making nouns, which is -기!

> **Ex)**
> 그 사람은 한국어를 배우기(를) 시작했어요.
> = He started learning Korean.

In this sentence, you can see that 한국어를 배우다 has been changed to the noun form of 한국어를 배우기 to be used as the object of 시작하다.

Track
17

Then, what is the difference between -(으)ㅁ and -기?

The basic difference between -(으)ㅁ and -기 is that the two endings are usually used with different types of verbs:

Verbs that follow nouns made using -(으)ㅁ	Verbs that follow nouns made using -기
옳다 (= to be right)	쉽다 (= to be easy)
나쁘다 (= to be bad/wrong)	어렵다 (= to be difficult)
분명하다 (= to be certain)	좋다 (= to like)
확실하다 (= to be sure)	싫다 (= to hate)
발견하다 (= to discover)	바라다 (= to hope)

59

알다 (= to know)	시작하다 (= to begin)
주장하다 (= to claim, to insist)	계속하다 (= to continue)
알리다 (= to tell/notify)	멈추다 (= to stop)
...etc.	약속하다 (= to promise)
	...etc.

The verbs in the left column are related to whether something is a fact, or whether it is the right or wrong thing to do.

Examples

Track 17

I am sure that he/she is a student.
= 학생임이 분명해요. (O)
   학생이기가 분명해요. (X)

Learning Korean is easy.
= 한국어를 배우기는 쉬워요. (O)
   한국어를 배움은 쉬워요. (X)

He is difficult to meet.
= 그 사람은 만나기가 어려워요. (O)
   그 사람은 만남이 어려워요. (X)

I proved that I am innocent.
= 무죄임을 증명했어요. (O)

무죄이기를 증명했어요. (X)

He claimed that he was innocent.
= 그 사람은 자신이 무죄임을 주장했어요.* (O)
  그 사람은 자신이 무죄이기를 주장했어요. (X)
* In this sentence, you can see the clause "자신이 무죄이다" inside the bigger structure "그 사람은 주장했어요."

3.
-(으)ㅁ can also be used at the end of a sentence when it is not clear which formality level or sentence ending one should use. This usage is often found in written memos, online messages, warnings, reports, dictionaries, laws, notices, etc.

Track 17

Ex)
진석진 씨에게 전화 왔음.
= Someone named 진석진 called you.

When you answer the phone for your coworker when she is away, you can leave a memo like this. You could write "전화 왔어요" or "전화 왔습니다", but since you are not really "talking" to your coworker but rather simply delivering information, you can just use the neutral -(으)ㅁ ending. This is neither 반말 nor 존댓말. However, you would not write this to someone who is older than you unless you are close with them.

Ex)
읽음.
= (It has been) read.

61

When you send a message to someone on your phone or write an email, when the recipient receives and reads the message your phone or email might say "읽음" to let you know that the person read it. -(으)ㅁ is used instead of "읽었어요" or "읽었습니다" because it is more neutral and shorter to use.

Ex)

모르고 있음.

= He does not know.

You can see this type of subtitle on Korean TV shows. If one person does not know a fact that everybody else knows, you might see "모르고 있음" or "아직 모르고 있음" written on the screen, which means, "He does not know" or, "He does not know yet."

Ex)

오늘 비가 옴.

= It rained today.

You might also use -(으)ㅁ in a journal as well if you list facts about the day rather than write a long passage.

Sample Dialogue

Track 18

예은: 주연 씨, 왜 얼음을 씹어 먹고 있어요?	*Ye-eun: Jooyeon, why are you chewing on ice?*
주연: 졸음 쫓으려고요.	*Jooyeon: To wake myself up.*
예은: 그렇게 졸려요?	*Ye-eun: Are you that sleepy?*
주연: 네, 사실 방금 졸다가 꿈까지 꿨어요.	*Jooyeon: Yes, I actually just nodded off and even had a dream.*

✏ *Exercises for Lesson* **9**

Change the following verbs into nouns by attaching -(으)ㅁ.

1. 웃다 →

2. 울다 →

3. 믿다 →

4. 알다 →

5. 살다 →

6. 추다 →

7. 자다 →

8. 젊다 →

9. 꾸다 →

10. 졸다 →

Check the answers on **p. 217**

LESSON **10**

Sentence Building Drill 15

Sentence Building Drill 15

Track 19

In this series, we focus on how you can use the grammatical rules and expressions that you have learned previously to train yourself to comfortably make Korean sentences.

We will start off with THREE key sentences and practice changing different parts of these sentences so that you do not end up simply memorizing the same three sentences. We want you to be able to make Korean sentences as flexibly as possible.

Key Sentence (1)
버스에서 내리다가 전화기를 떨어뜨려 버렸어요.

= I accidentally dropped my phone while I was getting off the bus.

Key Sentence (2)
안 사려고 했는데, 50% 할인이라고 해서 사고 말았어요.

= I was not going to buy it, but they said it was 50% off so I ended up buying it.

Key Sentence (3)

이 대학교의 학생임을 증명할 수 있는 서류를 지참해야 함.

= You must bring a document that can prove that you are a student of this university.

Expansion & Variation Practice with Key Sentence (1)

0. Original Sentence:

버스에서 내리다가 전화기를 떨어뜨려 버렸어요.

= I accidentally dropped my phone while I was getting off the bus.

1.

버스에서 내리다가 = while I was getting off the bus / I was getting off the bus and...

길을 걷다가 = while I was walking / I was walking and...

책을 읽다가 = while I was reading a book / I was reading a book and...

창문을 열다가 = while I was opening the window / I was opening the window and...

2.

전화기를 떨어뜨려 버렸어요. = I accidentally dropped my phone.

전화기가 고장 나 버렸어요. = My phone broke (and I am not happy about it).

영화가 벌써 끝나 버렸어요. = The movie ended already (and I am surprised and not happy about it).

주연 씨가 사람들한테 말해 버렸어요. = Jooyeon told people (and she was not supposed to).

Expansion & Variation Practice with Key Sentence (2)

0. Original Sentence:

안 사려고 했는데, 50% 할인이라고 해서 사고 말았어요.

= I was not going to buy it, but they said it was 50% off so I ended up buying it.

1.

안 사려고 했는데 = I was not going to buy it but...

안 보려고 했는데 = I was not going to look at it but...

말 안 하려고 했는데 = I was not going to tell them but...

빨리 가려고 했는데 = I was going to be there early but...

2.

Track 19

50% 할인이라고 해서 = they said it was 50% off so...

건강에 좋다고 해서 = they said it was good for your health so...

오늘 할인이 끝난다고 해서 = they said the discount was ending today so...

이 영화가 재미있다고 해서 = they said this movie is good so...

3.

사고 말았어요. = I ended up buying it (I should not have).

들키고 말았어요. = I got busted (I did not want to).

먹고 말았어요. = I ended up eating it (I should not have).

늦고 말았어요. = I got there late (I should not have).

Expansion & Variation Practice with Key Sentence (3)

0. Original Sentence:

이 대학교의 학생임을 증명할 수 있는 서류를 지참해야 함.

= You must bring a document that can prove that you are a student of this university.

1.

이 대학교의 학생임 = (the fact that) you are a student of this university

이 방법이 최선임 = (the fact that) this method is the best

업무를 완료했음 = (the fact that) you have completed a task

바깥에서 보이지 않음 = (the fact that) it is not visible from the outside

2.

Track
19

서류를 지참해야 함 = you must bring a document

오전 9시까지 보내야 함 = you must send it by 9 a.m.

오늘과 내일은 가게 문을 닫음 = the store is closed today and tomorrow

100명이 참가했음 = 100 people attended

Sample Dialogue

Track
20

주연: 석진 씨, 표정이 왜 그래요? 괜찮아요?

석진: 화장실 가려고 했는데, "6시 이후에는
　　　이용할 수 없음"이라고 붙어 있었어요.

주연: 진짜요? 그래서 6시 되자마자 화장실 문을
　　　잠가 버린 거예요?

석진: 네. 다행히 저쪽에도 화장실이 있다고 해서
　　　가 보려고요.

*Jooyeon: Seokjin, why are you making that face?
　　　Are you okay?*

*Seokjin: I was going to go to the restroom, but
　　　there's a sign that says "Closed after 6
　　　o'clock".*

*Jooyeon: Really? So as soon as it's 6 o'clock, they
　　　lock the doors?*

*Seokjin: Yes. Luckily, they said there's a
　　　bathroom over there too, so I'm going
　　　to try going over there.*

69

✏ Exercises for Lesson 10

Translate each sentence into Korean and write it on the lines provided.

1. Jooyeon told people (and she was not supposed to).

....

2. I ended up buying it (I should not have).

....

Check the answers on **p. 217**

Write the syllable that best fills in the two blanks.

3. 이 대학교의 학생＿＿＿ = (the fact that) you are a student of this university

이 방법이 최선＿＿＿ = (the fact that) this method is the best

Answer: (   )

4. 업무를 완료했＿＿＿ = (the fact that) you have completed a task

바깥에서 보이지 않＿＿＿ = (the fact that) it is not visible from the outside

Answer: (   )

5. 서류를 지참해야＿＿＿ = you must bring a document

오전 9시까지 보내야＿＿＿ = you must send it by 9 a.m.

Answer: (   )

70

Traditional Korean Hat:
Gat (갓)

If you are anything like me, you often find yourself browsing through the ever-changing selection of movies and TV shows on Netflix when you have nothing else to do. Since I live in Korea, Korean movies and TV shows are often on my recommended list. This past year while browsing the new titles, I came across a TV show named *Kingdom* that grabbed my attention. It stars Bae Doo-Na, who I really enjoyed in another TV show called *Stranger*, which I also recommend checking out if you have not seen it yet. The other reason I wanted to check out *Kingdom* was because of its interesting premise about a zombie-like disease set during the Joseon period.

I am all for a good zombie film, and setting it in a time before modern technology puts a neat spin on things. And I am not the only one who really liked this series as many across the world were raving about it. It was so popular that multiple seasons were made.

However, one thing in particular stood out among all the zombie attacks and beautiful cinematography—the hats! People across the world wanted to know more about those gat (갓) hats the men were wearing. If you have watched the show, you know exactly what I am talking about. If not, no worries because I am going to go over some of the many hats you might have seen on the show or on other similar shows. Because let us face it, if you have made it this far, then chances are you have seen your fair share of Korean period films and TV shows.

So, what is a gat? A gat is a hat made of horsehair or bamboo that was worn by adult men during the Joseon Dynasty. Technically, the category of 갓 also includes conical bamboo hats without a brim. However, in general, 갓 usually refers to a type of hat called heukrip (흑립), which are black and almost completely transparent, and have a wide brim with a bamboo frame. Above the brim, the hat rises up in a cylinder shape. During the 19th century, only nobility could wear this type of hat. These hats were a way of showing social status while protecting the wearer's sangtu (상투), or topknot.

So, what about the lower classes? What did they wear? People who were not nobility typically wore a hat woven from split bamboo called paeraengi (패랭이). In 1895, however, wearing paeraengi was banned, and those in the lower classes were told to also wear heukrip. However, it is said that they did not dare to wear them.

If you have seen the show *Kingdom*, you know that these are not the only types of hats people wore. Depending on their occupation, people wore different types of hats. For example, another hat worn by men was the dongpagwan (동파관). This hat was made from horsehair and was worn by scholars and government officials. It had two layered panels on the front and the back.

Another hat that was worn during this period was called a samo (사모). This hat was worn by government officials and indicated the rank of the official. It had flaps on the back that came out horizontally on the sides.

There is one more interesting fact about traditional hats that I would like to tell you about. During this time, there was a type of hat called baekrip (백립), which referred to basically any hat that was white. These hats were special because they were only worn during times of mourning. In fact, people wore all white when mourning the passing of a loved one. Even today, you can still sometimes see what remains of this custom. Women in mourning will wear white bows in their hair, and men will wear a white band around their arm.

Now, I have only touched the surface of the hats that used to be worn here in Korea. There are many more. With this blog, I hope that I have piqued your interest about the different types of hats that the men of Korea used to wear. Next time you watch a Korean period piece, try to spot the different hats and see if you can guess the rank or position of the character.

Written by Johnny Bland

우와!

벌써 Lesson 10까지 공부했네요!
다음 레슨에는 어떤 재미있는 표현이 기다리고 있을까요?

LESSON **11**

Advanced Idiomatic Expressions 8

마음 (Heart, Mind)

This is an Advanced Idiomatic Expressions lesson related to 마음, the heart or mind. In order to fully understand and use the expressions introduced in this series, it is essential that you understand the grammatical structure of the sentences. When you come across a grammar point that you are unfamiliar with, please go back and review the related TTMIK lessons.

Track
21

Keyword: **마음** = heart, mind

I. **마음을 먹다** = to make up one's mind

  ▷ **먹다** = to eat

Literally translated, 마음을 먹다 means "to eat one's mind" but the actual meaning is to determine or make up one's mind. You can use this expression when you are talking about your determination to do something, although it does not necessarily guarantee that you will actually do it. This expression is used so often that it has become one word, so you can drop the object marker, 을, and write it without a space, 마음먹다.

77

Ex)

이번에는 정말로 운동을 매일 하기로 마음먹었어요.

= I have made up my mind this time to really exercise every day.

* 마음먹다 is often used with "verb stem + -기로".

2. 마음대로 하다 = to do as one wants

You can use this phrase to describe how one does things the way they want to, or how one can choose to do whatever they want to do. You can say "마음대로 하세요" to someone to say, "Do whatever you want" or, "Do as you please" but if you want to be more polite you can say "편하신 대로 하세요", which literally means, "Do it the way that is comfortable for you."

Ex)

저는 그 책 필요 없으니까 마음대로 하세요.

= I do not need that book so do whatever you want with it.

3. 마음에 들다 = to like, to find something likeable
▷ 들다 = to go in

마음에 들다 is literally translated as "to enter one's heart" and means that you find something likeable. The difference between 좋아하다 and 마음에 들다 is that you say 좋아하다 about something that you have already liked for some time, whereas 마음에 들다 is usually used for things that you see for the first time and decide that you like. 마음에 들다 can be used for people as well as things.

Ex)

마음에 드는 가방 있어요?

= Is there a bag that you like?

* Based on the difference between 좋아하다 and 마음에 들다 that was mentioned earlier, Korean speakers immediately know that this person is talking about a bag to buy rather than choosing one that they like among the bags that they already own.

4. 마음에 걸리다 = to weigh upon one's mind, to trouble one's mind
▷ 걸리다 = to be stuck, to be hung

걸다 means to hang something up or to lock a door, and 걸리다 is the passive voice of 걸다. So when you say that something is hung or hooked in your mind, it means that something is stuck in your head and is troubling you because you are either worried or feel bad about it.

Track 21

Ex)

어제 있었던 일이 마음에 걸려요.

= I keep thinking about what happened yesterday because I feel bad about it.

5. 마음에 두다 = to have something/someone on one's mind
▷ 두다 = to put something somewhere

When used in a negative way, this phrase is similar to 마음에 걸리다, but it has less of a feeling of being worried and can also refer to many other types of emotions too. You can be worried, upset, or even distracted by something. It is often used in the form 마음에 두지 마세요 to tell someone to forget about what happened or what someone said, mainly because it will not help to think about it or because it was unimportant. When used in a positive way, on the other hand, this phrase is often used when you have someone or something on your mind because you are interested in it.

Ex)

예지 씨가 한 말은 너무 마음에 두지 마세요.

= Do not think about what Yeji said.

= Pay no attention to what Yeji said.

6. 마음에 없는 말을 하다 = to say something without meaning it

▷ 없다 = to not exist, to not have

▷ 말 = words, language, speech

When you say something that is not "in your heart" or "in your mind", it means that you are saying something that you do not really mean or are not serious about. You can hear this expression often when someone is offering too many compliments, or when someone offers to do something they probably will not follow through with.

Ex)

마음에도 없는 말 하지 마세요.

= Do not say what you do not even mean.

* People often say 마음에도 없는 말 instead of 마음에 없는 말 for emphasis, similar to how the word "even" is used in English.

7. 마음은 굴뚝 같다 = to wish one could do something right now, to want to do something right but be unable to do it

▷ 굴뚝 = chimney

▷ 같다 = to be like

When you say that your heart is like a chimney, it does not mean that you are tough, hot-tempered, or warm. In this context, you can think of the 굴뚝 as a place where the result of something comes out. In this case, smoke is the result, and is caused by boiling water or burning wood. So by saying 마음은 굴뚝 같다, you are implying that your mind is already focused on results, even though you have not started, or will not be able to start doing something. You can say this when you really want to do something but you cannot, or when you want to be polite about something you cannot do.

Ex)

도와주고 싶은 마음은 굴뚝 같지만, 오늘은 너무 바빠요.

= I would love to help you, but I am really busy today.

8. 마음이 놓이다 = to feel relieved

▷ 놓다 = to put down, to let go

▷ 놓이다 = (for something) to be let go

When you are worried about something, your mind is not at ease and cannot fully rest. So 마음이 놓이다 describes how one's mind is finally put to rest, instead of being filled with anxiety.

Ex)

그 말을 들으니까 마음이 놓이네요.

= I feel relieved to hear that.

9. 마음이 통하다 = to understand each other well

▷ 통하다 = to go through, to flow through, to circulate

81

When two people have a strong connection with each other, they know each other well and are comfortable around one another. You can use the verb 통하다 for languages as well, like when you ask if English is spoken/understood in Korea. "한국에서 영어 통해요?" means, "Is English understood in Korea?"

Ex)

마음이 통하는 친구들이랑 여행하면 너무 재미있어요.

= Traveling with friends that you connect with and relate well to is a lot of fun.

10. **마음이 무겁다** = to have a heavy heart, to feel bad

▷ **무겁다** = to be heavy

Track
21

This expression is similar in English as well. When you have a heavy heart, you feel bad about someone's situation, or about what you said or did to someone.

Ex)

저 때문에 경기에서 진 것 같아서 마음이 무겁습니다.

= I feel bad because it looks like we lost the game because of me.

Sample Dialogue

Track 22

경은: 어제 경화 씨가 한 말이 계속 마음에
걸려요.

현우: 너무 경은 씨 마음대로 한다는 말이요?

경은: 네. 마음이 너무 무겁네요.

현우: 너무 마음에 두지 말아요. 경화 씨가
어제 화가 많이 나서 그렇게 말했지만
진심은 아닐 거예요.

Kyeong-eun: I keep thinking about what Kyung-hwa said yesterday.

Hyunwoo: That she said you do things your own way too much?

Kyeong-eun: Yes. I feel bad about it.

Hyunwoo: Don't think about it too much. Kyung-hwa was really angry yesterday so she said that but she probably didn't mean it.

✏ Exercises for Lesson 11

Check the answers on p. 217

Fill in the blanks with the appropriate idioms with 마음 *from this lesson.*

1. (   )

 = to feel relieved

2. (   )

 = to understand each other well

3. (   )

 = to weigh upon one's mind, to trouble one's mind

4. (   )

 = to say something without meaning it

5. (   )

 = to make up one's mind

LESSON **12**

To look/seem + adjective

-아/어/여 보이다

Let us look at how to say that someone or something "seems" to be in a certain state or "looks" a certain way. The basic structure, -아/어/여 보이다, is fairly easy to understand and use, but it is important to know the difference between this structure and other similar structures.

Track
23

> ### *Conjugation*
>
> **Verb stem + -아/어/여 보이다**
>
> * 보이다 is originally the passive voice of 보다, to see.

Ex)

재미있다 = to be fun

재미있 + -어 보이다 = 재미있어 보이다 = to look fun, to look interesting

재미있어 보여요. = It looks fun.

재미있어 보여요? = Does it look fun?

85

Sample Sentences

피곤해 보여요.

= You look tired.

피곤해 보여요. 좀 쉬세요.

= You look tired. Take a break.

피곤해 보여요. 어제 못 잤어요?

= You look tired. Did you not sleep well last night?

이 영화는 재미없어 보여요.

= This movie looks boring.

Track 23

이거 매워 보이는데, 사실은 하나도 안 매워요.

= This looks spicy, but it is not spicy at all.

이 케이크가 맛있어 보여서 샀는데, 너무 달아요.

= This cake looked delicious so I bought it, but it is too sweet.

사장님 기분이 안 좋아 보이는데, 무슨 일 있어요?

= The boss does not look happy. Is there something wrong?

Difference between 좋아 보이네요 and 좋은 것 같아요

When -아/어/여 보이다 and -(으)ㄴ 것 같다 are used to talk about living things, such as people or animals, they have pretty much the same meaning.

Ex)

사장님 기분이 안 좋아 보이는데, 무슨 일 있어요?

= The boss does not look happy. Is there something wrong?

사장님 기분이 안 좋은 것 같은데, 무슨 일 있어요?

= I think the boss is upset. Is there something wrong?

However, when using -아/어/여 보이다 and -(으)ㄴ 것 같다 to refer to nonliving things, the usage between the two differs slightly. -아/어/여 보이다 can be used before and after someone finds out about or experiences something, whereas -(으)ㄴ 것 같다 can only be used after someone finds out about or experiences something. If you want to use 것 같다 before you find out about or experience something, you can use -(으)ㄹ 것 같다.

Track 23

Ex)

이 가방 비싸 보여요.

= This bag looks expensive. (You do not know the price yet.)

= This bag looks expensive (even though it is actually not).

이 가방 비싼 것 같아요.

= I think this bag is expensive. (You know how much the bag costs.)

이 가방 비쌀 것 같아요.

= I think this bag must be expensive.

이거 매워 보이는데, 사실은 하나도 안 매워요.

= This looks spicy (before you eat it), but it is not spicy at all.

이거 매울 것 같았는데, 사실은 하나도 안 매웠어요.

= I thought it would be spicy but it was not spicy at all.

Using 보이다 with nouns

With nouns, instead of using -아/어/여 after a verb stem, you must first add -처럼 or -같이 after the noun.

Ex)
학생 = student
학생처럼 보여요. = He looks like a student.
학생 같아요. = He looks like a student, so I think he is a student. / He acts like a student.

Sample Sentences

Track 23

비둘기처럼 보이네요.
= It looks like a pigeon.

멀어서 잘 안 보이지만, 3처럼 보이네요.
= I cannot see clearly because it is far, but it looks like a three.

경찰처럼 보이는 사람이 그 여자를 데려갔어요.
= Someone who looks like a cop took her.

Sample Dialogue

Track 24

경은: 예지 씨, 오늘 엄청 피곤해 보여요.

예지: 그래요? 사실은 어제 개봉한 영화 빨리 보고 싶어서 오늘 새벽에 보고 출근했거든요. 그래서 좀 피곤해요.

경은: 아, 그랬구나. 영화는 재미있었어요?

예지: 별로 재미없었어요. 예고편만 봤을 때는 재밌어 보였는데 그게 다였어요.

Kyeong-eun: Yeji, you look really tired today.

Yeji: Do I? Actually I really wanted to see a movie that premiered yesterday, so I saw it early in the morning before coming to work. So I'm a bit tired.

Kyeong-eun: Oh, I see. Was the movie good?

Yeji: It wasn't very good. It looked good in the trailer but that was it.

✏️ Exercises for Lesson 12

Translate each sentence into Korean using -아/어/여 보이다 *and write it on the lines provided.*

1. You look tired.

....

2. This looks spicy.

....

3. This movie looks boring.

....

4. The boss does not look happy.

  * boss = 사장님

....

5. This cake looked delicious so I bought it, but it is too sweet.

....

LESSON **13**

Word Builder 19

신(新)

Track
25

Word Builder lessons are designed to help you understand how to expand your vocabulary by learning and understanding some common and basic building blocks of Korean words. The words and letters introduced through Word Builder lessons are not necessarily all Chinese characters, or 한자, and although many of them are based on Chinese characters, their meanings can differ from modern-day Chinese. Your goal, through these lessons, is to understand how Korean words are formed and remember key word elements to expand your Korean vocabulary from there. You certainly do not have to memorize the Hanja characters to do this, but if you want to, feel free!

Today's key word element is 신.

The Chinese character for this is 新. There are many other Chinese characters (or Hanja letters) that are used for 신, so keep in mind that not all words that have 신 in them have related meanings.

The word 신 (新) is related to "new".

신 (new) + 제 (make) + 품 (item) = 신제품 新製品 = new product

신 (new) + 기록 (record) = 신기록 新記錄 = new record

신 (new) + 학 (learn, school) + 기 (period) = 신학기 新學期 = new semester

신 (new) + 인 (person) = 신인 新人 = rookie

* This is used a lot in the entertainment industry and in the sports industry.

Track 25

Ex)
신인 배우 新人 俳優 = new actor
신인 가수 新人 歌手 = new singer
신인 선수 新人 選手 = rookie player

신 (new) + 작 (make) = 신작 新作 = new movie/book/musical, etc.

신 (new) + 혼 (marriage) = 신혼 新婚 = newlywed, the first few years of married life

갱 (alter) + 신 (new) = 갱신 更新 = modification, renewal

경 (alter) + 신 (new) = 경신 更新 = breaking a record

Ex)
신기록 경신 新記錄 更新 = setting a new record

혁 (alter) + 신 (new) = 혁신 革新 = innovation

신 (new) + 세대 (generation) = 신세대 新世代 = new generation

Related Vocabulary
구세대 舊世代 = old generation

신 (new) + 세계 (world) = 신세계 新世界 = new world

신 (new) + 입 (enter) = 신입 新入 = new employee

신 (new) + 입 (enter) + 사 (company) + 원 (member) = 신입 사원 新入 社員 = new employee

신 (new) + 입 (enter) + 생 (student) = 신입생 新入生 = freshman student
* For both 신입 사원 and 신입생, people often use the shortened version, 신입.

Track 25

신 (new) + 병 (soldier) = 신병 新兵 = rookie soldier

신 (new) + 간 (publish) = 신간 新刊 = new publication

신 (new) + 간 (publish) + 서 (book) + 적 (document) = 신간 서적 新刊 書籍 = newly published book
* 서적 is a more formal word for 책.

Sample Dialogue

Track 26

진우: 재은 씨, 이거 보세요. 최진영 작가 신간 나왔어요.

재은: 아! 진우 씨가 좋아한다고 했던 그 신인 작가요?

진우: 네. 이 책이 지금 인기가 엄청 많아서 매일 판매 기록을 경신하고 있대요.

재은: 오, 그래요? 저도 읽고 싶네요. 진우 씨 다 읽으면 저 좀 빌려주세요.

진우: 네, 알겠어요.

Jinwoo: Jae-eun, look at this. Jinyoung Choi's new book came out.

Jae-eun: Oh! Is that the new writer you said you like?

Jinwoo: Yes. This book is so popular right now that they say it's breaking sales records every day.

Jae-eun: Oh, really? I want to read it, too. When you're done reading it, please lend it to me.

Jinwoo: Okay.

✎ Exercises for Lesson 13

Fill in the blanks with the appropriate Sino-Korean word from the lesson.

1. The key word element (   ) is related to "new".

2. (   ) = newlywed, the first few years of married life

3. (   ) = freshman student

4. (   ) = new record

5. (   ) = new generation

Check the answers on **p. 217**

LESSON **14**

Advanced Situational Expressions 10

후회할 때
(When You Regret Something)

Track 27

Welcome to another lesson in the Advanced Situational Expressions series. Throughout this series, we take a look at common situations and some of the advanced expressions you can use in each of them. In this lesson, we will introduce various expressions that are related to regretting something or having feelings of regret.

1.

후회가 돼요.

= I regret it.

* Even though there is a verb in the active voice that means "to regret", 후회하다, people often use the passive voice when they regret something. With this usage, you are not actively regretting something, but rather acknowledging that you regret what happened.

2.

후회가 막심해요. (formal expression)

= I deeply regret it.

* 막심하다 means "to be serious", but it is only used in specific phrases, such as "손해가

막심하다 (the loss is serious)" or "피해가 막심하다 (the damage is serious)".

3.

어렸을 때 더 많이 놀지 않은 게 후회가 돼요.

= I regret not having played more when I was little.

4.

그 이야기를 꺼낸 것 자체가 후회스러워요.

= I regret the fact that I even brought that up.

* 자체 = in itself, in and of itself

** 후회스럽다 = to be regretful

5.

말하지 말았어야 했어요.

= I should not have told them.

* Verb + -지 말았어야 했어요 = (someone) should not have done (something)

Track
27

Ex)

웃지 말았어야 했어요. = I should not have laughed.

6.

이거 괜히 샀어요.

= I should not have bought it.

* 괜히 = in vain, uselessly

Ex)

괜히 했어요. = I should not have done that.

괜히 팔았어요. = I should not have sold it.

괜히 왔어요. = I should not have come here.

7.

오지 말걸 그랬어요.

= I should not have come here.

* This sentence is short for 오지 말 것을 그랬어요, and it has the nuance that you had the option to not come, but you came anyway, and you regret it.

** -지 말걸 그랬어요 is similar to -지 말았어야 했어요, but when you say "verb ＋ -지 말았어야 했어요", you might be upset because you did something even though you were not supposed to. However, if you say "verb ＋ -지 말걸 그랬어요", you just think that it might have been better if you had not done it.

*** You can even drop the 그랬어요 part and simply say, -지 말걸.

> **Ex)**
> 오지 말걸. = I should not have come here.
> 말하지 말걸. = I should not have told them.
> 사지 말걸. = I should not have bought it.

8.

좀 더 일찍 도착했더라면 좋았을 텐데요.

= It would have been nice if we had arrived a little earlier.

* The structure is "verb ＋ -았/었/였더라면 좋았을 텐데요".

** People drop -요 when they say to themselves, such as "좀 더 일찍 도착했더라면 좋았을 텐데." You can even drop the 좋았을 텐데 part and say "좀 더 일찍 도착했더라면."

9.

그냥 우리끼리 하는 게 나을 뻔했어요.

= It might have been better to just have done it by ourselves.

* The structure is "verb ＋ -는 게 나을 뻔했어요".

10.

그래서 후회 중이에요.

= Therefore, I am regretting it now.

11.

원래 그럴 생각은 없었어요.

= I did not intend to do it.

* You can use this to show your regret, to apologize, or to make an excuse.

12.

지금 와서 생각해 보면, 제가 그때 왜 그랬나 싶어요.

= Looking back now, I wonder why I did that back then.

* The structure is "왜 verb + -았/었/였나 싶어요", and it is commonly used with the phrase, 지금 와서 생각해 보면.

Track 27

Sample Dialogue

Track 28

승우: 신입 사원 때부터 저금을 열심히 했어야
했는데... 통장 잔고 보니까 후회가
막심해요.

우현: 그래요? 저는 이십 대 때 더 많이 놀지
않은 게 후회돼요.

승우: 우현 씨는 월급 받으면 거의 다
저금했죠?

우현: 네, 맞아요. 지금 와서 생각해 보면, 제가
그때 왜 그랬나 싶어요.

Seungwoo: I should have started saving money
when I first began working... Looking at
the balance in my account now, I deeply
regret not doing so.

Woohyun: Do you? I regret not having more fun in
my twenties.

Seungwoo: You saved most of your earnings from
your paychecks, right?

Woohyun: That's right. Thinking about it now, I'm
wondering why I did that.

🖉 *Exercises for Lesson 14*

Fill in the blanks with the appropriate expression from the lesson. They are all in **존댓말**.

1. 후회가 (   ). (formal expression)

= I deeply regret it.

2. 오지 (   ) 그랬어요.

= I should not have come here.

3. 이거 (   ) 샀어요.

= I should not have bought it.

4. 좀 더 일찍 도착했더라면 (   ).

= It would have been nice if we had arrived a little earlier.

5. 그냥 우리끼리 하는 게 (   ).

= It might have been better to just have done it by ourselves.

6. 지금 와서 생각해 보면, 제가 그때 왜 그랬나 (   ).

= Looking back now, I wonder why I did that back then.

Check the answers on **p. 217**

LESSON **15**

Advanced Idiomatic Expressions 9

기분 (Feeling)

Track
29

This is an Advanced Idiomatic Expressions lesson related to 기분, feelings or emotions. In order to fully understand and use the expressions introduced in this series, it is essential that you understand the grammatical structure of the sentences. When you come across a grammar point that you are unfamiliar with, please go back and review the related TTMIK lessons.

Keyword: 기분 = feeling, emotion, mood

I. **기분이 좋다** = to feel happy, to feel upbeat

▷ **좋다** = to be good

When your 기분 (feeling) is good, it means that you are feeling great and happy in general. When you say that you feel good in English, it can also be related to your health, but in Korean, it is mostly related to your feelings at that moment. You can also use 기분이 좋다 when you feel good because of a cool breeze or a soothing massage, just not about your general health condition on a certain day.

Ex)

오늘 기분이 좋아 보이는데, 좋은 일 있어요?

= You look happy today. Is there something good happening?

2. 기분이 나쁘다 = to be in a bad mood, to feel unpleasant

▷ 나쁘다 = to be bad

When you say that you "feel bad" in English, it can mean that you are sorry about something and you want to apologize or you feel responsible for a bad result. But in Korean, when you say 기분이 나쁘다, it never means that you are apologetic. Rather, it indicates that you are feeling upset or unpleasant. You can also say 기분이 나쁘다 about something or someone that you find unpleasant.

Track
29

Ex)

그 사람이 저를 보고 웃으면 왠지 기분이 나빠요.

= When he smiles at me, for some reason, it feels unpleasant.

3. 기분 좋게 = willingly, with good cheer

▷ 좋게 = nicely

기분 좋게 is basically the adverbial form of 기분 좋다. It can be used to either describe how someone does something willingly without feeling forced or upset about having to do it, or to describe how someone is actually feeling happy while doing something. If you say 기분 좋게 만들다, it means "to make someone feel good".

Ex)

원래는 기분 좋게 도와주려고 했는데, 기분 나빠졌어요. 혼자 하세요.

= At first I was going to help you cheerfully, but I feel angry now. You can do it by yourself.

4. 기분을 풀다 = to relieve or resolve one's feelings

풀다 literally means to "resolve" or "untangle" something, so when you untangle someone's feelings of being upset, you make them feel better or less upset. You can also use 기분을 풀다 to describe how you divert yourself and relieve stress.

Track 29

Ex)

제가 맛있는 거 사 줄 테니까 이제 기분 좀 풀어요.

= I will buy you something delicious, so please stop being angry at me.

5. -(으)ㄹ 기분이 아니다 = to be not in the mood for

This expression is very similar to the English expression, "to be not in the mood" to do something.

Ex)

저 지금 농담할 기분 아니에요.

= I am not in the mood to joke (with you).

지금 피자 먹을 기분이 아니에요.

= I am not in the mood to eat pizza.

6. 기분이 상하다 = to be offended

▷ 상하다 = to rot, to go bad

* 상하다 is often used with food to mean that it is rotten or has gone bad.

You can use 기분이 상하다 when someone's feelings are hurt by what someone else said, or when someone is offended by something that happened.

Ex)

그냥 농담이었는데 기분 상했어요?

= I was just joking. Did I hurt your feelings?

7. 기분 내키는 대로 = just the way one wants

▷ 내키다 = to feel like, to be inclined

▷ -(으/느)ㄴ 대로 = the way something goes

Track 29

The expression 기분 내키는 대로 has a slightly negative connotation, so when you say it about someone, you are usually not very happy about the way that person behaves.

Ex)

그 사람은 기분 내키는 대로 행동하는 게 꼭 어린아이 같아요.

= He does whatever he feels like, just like a child.

8. 기분이 들뜨다 = to be excited, to be exhilarated

▷ 들뜨다 = to be excited

Ex)

내일 런던에 갈 생각에 기분이 들떴어요.

= I am very excited by the thought of going to London tomorrow.

9. 기분 전환을 하다 = to refresh oneself

전환 means transition or change, so when you "do" a "기분 전환 (mood transition)", it usually means that you refresh yourself or get some fresh air, usually by doing something different like going for a walk, meeting friends, or going on a short trip. 전환 is often used with 기분, and not by itself.

Track 29

Ex)

기분 전환 하러 잠시 밖에 나갔다 왔어요.

= I went out for a bit to refresh myself.

10. 기분 탓이다 = to be just one's imagination

▷ 탓 = reason, fault, blame

When there is no real issue or substantial problem but you feel like something is wrong or something is happening, you can say that it is just the fault of your 기분 (feeling). You can often hear people saying "기분 탓인가? (= It is just me?)" or "기분 탓일 거예요 (= You are just feeling that way)".

Ex)

그냥 기분 탓일 거예요. 너무 걱정 마세요.

= You are just imagining things. Do not worry too much.

11. -(으/느)ㄴ 기분이 들다 = to feel that..., to have a feeling that...

▷ 들다 = to come in

기분이 들다 literally means "a feeling enters" so when you get the feeling that something is happening or will happen, you can use this phrase.

Ex)
왠지 오늘은 좋은 일이 있을 것 같은 기분이 들어요.

= For some reason, I feel like something good is going to happen (to me).

12. 기분이 가라앉다 = to feel down

▷ 가라앉다 = to sink

Track 29

In English, if you say "I feel down", it sounds like you were already feeling down before you said it out loud. However, in Korean, if you say 가라앉다, you are emphasizing that you were feeling good but now you feel down.

Ex)
그 얘기를 들으니 기분이 가라앉았어요.

= After hearing that news, I felt down.

Sample Dialogue

예지: 저 스페인어 실력 많이 는 것 같지 않아요?

현우: 글쎄요. 기분 탓인 것 같은데요?

예지: 너무해요. 실력이 는 것 같아서 기분 좋았었는데, 그 말 듣고 기분이 가라앉았어요.

현우: 아, 죄송해요. 장난친 건데 혹시 기분 상했어요?

Yeji: Don't you think my Spanish has gotten a lot better?

Hyunwoo: I don't know. I think it might just be your imagination?

Yeji: That's too harsh. I thought I'd improved so I was happy, but hearing that I feel down.

Hyunwoo: Oh, I'm sorry. I was just kidding. Did I hurt your feelings?

✎ Exercises for Lesson 15

Fill in the blanks with the appropriate idioms with 기분 *from this lesson.*

1. (   )

    = to be offended

2. (   )

    = to relieve or resolve one's feelings

3. (   )

    = to refresh oneself

4. (   )

    = just the way one wants

5. (   )

    = to be excited, to be exhilarated

Check the answers on **p. 217**

LESSON 16

In return for, Since it will be…

-(으)ㄹ 테니(까)

Track 31

In this lesson, we are taking a look at the structure -(으)ㄹ 테니(까). This is often used in situations where one person wants, or asks, the other person to do something. When you use it after a verb stem that ends with a consonant, you add -을 테니(까). When the verb stem ends with a vowel, you add -ㄹ 테니(까). The original form is -을 테니까 or -ㄹ 테니까, but it is always interchangeable with -을 테니 or -ㄹ 테니, with the last syllable, 까, omitted.

Original meaning

-테니(까) comes from the combination of 터 and -이니(까). 터 means a "place", "site", "lot", "ground", or "foundation". You will often see 터 used in compound words, such as "놀이터 (playground)", "낚시터 (fishing spot)", "일터 (workplace)", etc.

There are two main usages for this structure:

1.

You can use this structure when you offer to do one thing, and ask the listener to do something else in return. What you ask of the other person does not always have to be a favor; it can also be something that you want them to do for their own good. Therefore, -(으)ㄹ 테니(까) is often translated as "I will do this, so in return, I want you to do this". As a result, you cannot use this structure in all situations where you say "therefore" or "so" in English.

> **Ex)**
> 이건 제가 할 테니까, 걱정하지 말고 쉬세요.
> = I will do this, so do not worry and get some rest.

In the sentence above, you are offering to take care of something and telling the other person to go get some rest. However, you cannot use this structure when referring to someone else doing something. For example, "이건 석진 씨가 할 테니까, 걱정하지 말고 쉬세요" is not a natural sentence. If you want to say something like, "Seokjin will take care of this, so do not worry" in Korean, you can either use the -(으)ㄹ 거니까 ending and say 석진 씨가 할 거니까, or you can keep yourself as the subject of the sentence by saying 이건 석진 씨한테 하라고 할 테니까, meaning "I will tell Seokjin to do this, so…"

2.

When you are making an assumption you are almost certain about, you can use this structure to mean "I assume/think/believe that this will happen/is happening, so let us do this/please do this." Even when you are talking about a present state or action, since you are making an assumption and therefore WILL have to check to see if you are right, the sentence is always in the future tense.

111

Ex)

밖에 추울 테니까 나가지 마세요.

= It is probably cold outside, so do not go out.

If you are NOT making an assumption and are just stating a known fact, you can use the -(으)니까 structure and just say "밖에 추우니까". The -(으)ㄹ 테니(까) structure is often used together in a sentence with -(으)면, which means "if". For example, if you say "지금 밖에 나가면 추울 테니까", it means "if you go outside now, it will probably be cold, so..."

Sometimes, -(으)ㄹ 테니까 can be shortened to -(으)ㄹ 테니, but -(으)ㄹ 테니까 is more commonly used when speaking.

Sample Sentences

Track 31

제가 점심 살 테니까, 경화 씨가 커피 사세요.

= I will buy lunch, so Kyung-hwa, you buy coffee.

저는 먼저 갈 테니까 나중에 오세요.

= I will go first, so you can come later.

나머지는 제가 할 테니까 먼저 퇴근하세요.

= I will do the rest, so please go home first.

저는 뛰어갈 테니까, 예지 씨는 택시 타고 오세요.

= I will run, so Yeji, you take a taxi.

갑자기 찾아가면 놀랄 테니까, 전화를 할까요?

= If we visit her suddenly she will probably be surprised, so shall we call her?

지금 출발하면 너무 일찍 도착할 테니까, 10분 뒤에 출발해요.

= If you leave now you will probably get there too early, so leave in 10 minutes.

아직 뜨거울 테니까 조심하세요.

= It is probably still hot, so be careful.

    * If someone says, "뜨거우니까 조심하세요", the person knows for a fact that it is hot, so they are telling you to be careful.

Track 31

Sample Dialogue

신욱: 민재야, 청소 지금 시작하자.

민재: 벌써? 알겠어.

신욱: 내가 바닥 청소를 할 테니까, 너는 창문을 닦아. 청소기가 어디 있었지?

민재: 지하실에 있어. 내가 꺼내 올 테니까 여기 있어.

Shinwook: Minjae, let's start cleaning now.

Minjae: Already? Okay.

Shinwook: I will clean the floor, so you wipe down the windows. Where was the vacuum cleaner?

Minjae: It's in the basement. I'll go get it, so you stay here.

✏ Exercises for Lesson 16

Fill in the blanks using -(으)ㄹ 테니(까).

1. (   ), 경화 씨가 커피 사세요.

   = I will buy lunch, so Kyung-hwa, you buy coffee.

2. (   ) 나중에 오세요.

   = I will go first, so you can come later.

3. (   ) 먼저 퇴근하세요.

   = I will do the rest, so please go home first.

4. (   ), 예지 씨는 택시 타고 오세요.

   = I will run, so Yeji, you take a taxi.

5. (   ) 조심하세요.

   = It is probably still hot, so be careful.

Check the answers on **p. 218**

LESSON 17

Since, Once, As long as

-(으/느)ㄴ 이상

Track 33

In this lesson, we are introducing the structure -(으/느)ㄴ 이상. The word 이상(以上) by itself, means "not lower than" or "from this point and above". When used in the form -(으/느)ㄴ 이상, it can mean that the preceding clause is a fact that makes the following clause something that can naturally be expected or something that is supposed to happen.

-(으/느)ㄴ 이상 can be used in both the past tense and in the present tense, but in the present tense it is used more often in writing than speaking.

Ex)
저도 이 회사의 직원인 이상, 이 행사에 꼭 참여해야 돼요.
= Since I am also an employee in this company, I must participate in this event.
* You can break this down into two parts and make it more simple by saying, "저도 이 회사의 직원이에요. 이 행사에 꼭 참여해야 돼요."

Therefore, especially in spoken language, the structure -(으/느)ㄴ 이상 is used more commonly in the past tense than in the present tense. When used in the past tense, it can

116

be translated to "since you have already done this, this is bound to happen" or "you have done this, so this has to be the way things are".

Ex)

이미 공식 발표를 한 이상, 이제 취소할 수는 없어요.

= Since we have already made a public announcement, we cannot cancel it now.

Sample Sentences

비행기를 탄 이상, 도착할 때까지 내릴 수 없어요.

= Now that you have boarded the airplane, you cannot get off until you arrive.

한번 시작한 이상, 중간에 포기할 수 없어요.

= Once you have started, you cannot quit in the middle.

Track
33

여기까지 온 이상, 포기하지 말고 열심히 하세요.

= Since you have come this far, do not give up and keep working hard.

출근을 안 할 수는 있지만, 출근을 한 이상, 일을 안 할 수는 없어요.

= I could just not go to work, but once I (actually) go to work, I have to work (lit: I cannot not do work).

이 방에 들어온 이상, 이 게임을 꼭 해야 돼요.

= Once you have come into this room, you must play this game.

Negative Forms

When -(으/느)ㄴ 이상 is used in a negative form, the sentence can take the meaning of "as

117

long as" or "unless". The clause following -(으/느)ㄴ 이상 usually describes a negative situation or is a negative statement.

(I) Negative form + -(으/느)ㄴ 이상

As there are various ways to form a negative sentence in Korean, this structure also works with various forms of negative verb endings.

Sample Sentences

비행기를 타지 않는 이상, 그렇게 빨리 갈 수가 없어요.

= Unless you take an airplane, you cannot get there that fast.

계산기를 쓰지 않는 이상, 이렇게 복잡한 계산은 못 해요.

= Unless I use a calculator, I cannot do such a complex calculation.

아주 아프지 않은 이상, 저는 수업에 빠지지 않아요.

= Unless I am very sick, I do not skip classes.

* Of course, you can say 아주 아프지 않으면 instead of 아주 아프지 않은 이상, but by using -(으/느)ㄴ 이상, your statement sounds stronger, more stressed, and more obligatory.

(2) Noun + -이/가 아닌 이상

With nouns, since you need to add the verb -이다 before you can conjugate it, you must add the structure -이/가 아닌 이상 after the noun.

Sample Sentences

여기 직원이 아닌 이상, 들어갈 수가 없어요.

= Unless you are a staff member here, you cannot go in.

* "여기 직원이 아니면 들어갈 수가 없어요" can also be used, but using -이/가 아닌

이상 makes the statement sound stronger.

가족이 아닌 이상, 그런 건 알 수가 없어요.

= Unless you are family, it is impossible to know such things.

중요한 일이 아닌 이상, 지금 이 시간에 나갈 수는 없어요.

= Unless it is something important, I cannot go out at this hour.

Track 33

Sample Dialogue

캐시: 다니엘 씨, 제이슨 씨가 육 개월 만에 한국어를 유창하게 할 수 있게 되었대요!

다니엘: 네? 천재가 아닌 이상, 그건 불가능해요.

캐시: 진짜래요. 천재인가 봐요.

다니엘: 부럽네요. 저도 일단 시작한 이상, 열심히 해 볼 거예요.

Cassie: Daniel, Jason said he learned how to speak Korean fluently in only six months!

Daniel: What? Unless he's a genius, that's impossible.

Cassie: He said he really did. I guess he's a genius.

Daniel: I'm jealous. Once I start too, I will do my best.

✏ *Exercises for Lesson* 17

Fill in the blanks using -(으/느)ㄴ 이상.

I. (   ), 중간에 포기할 수 없어요.

= Once you have started, you cannot quit in the middle.

2. (   ), 포기하지 말고 열심히 하세요.

= Since you have come this far, do not give up and keep working hard.

3. (   ), 저는 수업에 빠지지 않아요.

= Unless I am very sick, I do not skip classes.

4. (   ), 이 게임을 꼭 해야 돼요.

= Once you have come into this room, you must play this game.

5. (   ), 그런 건 알 수가 없어요.

= Unless you are family, it is impossible to know such things.

Check the answers on **p. 218**

LESSON 18

(To worry/think) that it might

-(으)ㄹ까 봐

Track
35

In this lesson, we are looking at how -(으)ㄹ까 보다 is used in a sentence. As you learned in Level 3 Lesson 4, you can add the ending -(으)ㄹ까 after a verb stem to express an assumption (e.g. "내일 비가 올까요? = Do you think it will rain tomorrow?"). With -(으)ㄹ까 보다, an assumption is also implied, but you can also express concern, the reason for a decision, or an inclination to do something.

Usages of -(으)ㄹ까 보다

I. Expressing worry or concern

> *Structure*
> Verb stem + -(으)ㄹ까 봐 + another verb

When you are worried about something that MIGHT happen, you can use -(으)ㄹ까 봐 to talk about what you did or are doing as a result of your concern. You use -(으)ㄹ까 봐 only

122

when talking about things that might happen, but not when talking about things that are already happening or will happen for sure. In this case, when you use -(으)ㄹ까 봐 with the word 걱정, you can omit 봐 and just say -(으)ㄹ까 걱정이에요 or -(으)ㄹ까 걱정했어요.

Sample Sentences

나중에 후회할까 봐 걱정돼요.

= 나중에 후회할까 걱정돼요.

= I am worried that I might regret it later.

늦을까 봐 걱정이에요.

= 늦을까 걱정이에요.

= I am worried that we might be late.

시험에 떨어질까 봐 걱정이에요.

= 시험에 떨어질까 걱정이에요.

= I am worried that I might fail the exam.

Track 35

차가 막힐까 봐 걱정이에요.

= 차가 막힐까 걱정이에요.

= I am worried that the traffic might be bad.

아이가 실망할까 봐 아직 말 못 했어요.

= I was worried that the child might be disappointed, so I did not tell him yet.

* When -(으)ㄹ까 봐 is used with words OTHER than 걱정, people usually do not drop 봐.

2. Explaining the reason for a decision based on an assumption

> ### *Structure*
> Verb stem + -(으)ㄹ까 봐 + another verb

When you decide to do something based on the assumption that it is a good decision, or that something in particular might happen, you can use -(으)ㄹ까 봐. In this case, you can also say -(으)ㄹ까 봐서 to mean the same thing. Please note that in this usage, you cannot drop 봐.

Track 35

Sample Sentences

택시로 가면 더 빠를까 봐 택시를 탔는데, 결국은 지각했어요.

= I took a taxi thinking that it might be faster, but I ended up being late.

　* You could also say 택시로 가면 빠를 것 같아서, which expresses a stronger degree of confidence in your assumption.

비가 올까 봐 우산을 가져왔는데 비가 안 오네요.

= I brought an umbrella thinking that it might rain, but it is not raining.

공부하다가 잠이 올까 봐 커피 사 왔어요.

= I bought some coffee in case I fall asleep while studying.

배고프실까 봐 간식 사 왔어요.

= I brought some snacks in case you were hungry.

　* If you are speaking to your friends, you can say, "배고플까 봐 간식 사 왔어."

이 책 필요하실까 봐 가져왔어요.

= I thought you might need this book, so I brought it.

　* You could also say 필요하실 것 같아서 or 필요하실 수도 있어서 instead of 필요하실까 봐.

3. Expressing one's inclination to do something

> ### *Structure*
> Verb stem + -(으)ㄹ까 봐(요)

You can also use -(으)ㄹ까 봐 when you want to talk about something that you are feeling inclined to do, although you have not fully decided whether or not to do it quite yet. In this case, you can also say -(으)ㄹ까 해(요) instead of -(으)ㄹ까 봐(요) to mean the same thing.

Sample Sentences

오늘은 좀 쉴까 봐요.

= I think maybe I should get some rest today.

친구들한테 물어볼까 봐요.

= I think maybe I should ask my friends.

그냥 환불받을까 봐요.

= I am thinking maybe I should just get a refund.

이걸로 살까 봐요.

= Maybe I should buy this one.

중국어를 공부해 볼까 봐요.

= I am thinking maybe I should try studying Chinese.

Track
35

125

Sample Dialogue

아빠: 아빠한테 줘. 아빠가 뚜껑 열어
     줄게.

딸: 아빠, 내가 혼자 못 할까 봐 그래?

아빠: 아니, 아빠는 혹시 네가 열다가
     다칠까 봐 그러지.

딸: 아! 걱정 마. 이 정도는 혼자 할 수
    있어.

Dad: Give it to me. I'll open the lid for you.

*Daughter: Dad, you're saying that because you
think I won't be able to do it myself?*

*Dad: No, I just worry that you might hurt
yourself opening it.*

*Daughter. Ah! Don't worry. I can do this much
by myself.*

✐ Exercises for Lesson *18*

Fill in the blanks using **-(으)ㄹ까 봐**.

1. (   ) 걱정돼요.

   = I am worried that I might regret it later.

2. (   ) 걱정이에요.

   = I am worried that the traffic might be bad.

3. (   ) 아직 말 못 했어요.

   = I was worried that the child might be disappointed, so I did not tell him yet.

4. (   ) 간식 사 왔어요.

   = I brought some snacks in case you were hungry.

5. (   ) 가져왔어요.

   = I thought you might need this book, so I brought it.

Check the answers on **p. 218**

LESSON 19

Advanced Situational Expressions II

오랜만에 만났을 때
(When You Meet Someone After A Long Time)

Track 37

Welcome to another lesson in the Advanced Situational Expressions series. Throughout this series, we take a look at common situations and some of the advanced expressions you can use in each of them. In this Advanced Situational Expressions lesson, we are going to take a look at some expressions you can use or expect to hear when you meet someone after not seeing them for a long time.

1.

오랜만이에요.

= Long time no see.

* Between friends, you can just say "오랜만" or "오랜만이야."

2.

이게 얼마 만이에요.

= It has been a long time.

3.

얼마 만에 보는 거죠?

= How long has it been since we last met?

4.

별일 없죠?

= Everything alright?

* You might feel the need to answer in detail, but you can also just reply, "네, 별일 없어요."

5.

요새 어떻게 지내요?

= How are you doing these days?

6.

지난번에 본 게 벌써 2년 전이에요?

= The last time we met was already two years ago?

* You can change the verb 보다 to other verbs like 만나다 or 모이다.

Ex)
지난번에 만난 게 벌써 2년 전이에요?

7.

작년 가을에 보고 못 봤죠?

= We have not seen each other since last fall, right?

* You can replace 작년 가을 with other time related words, such as 지난주, 작년, 3년 전, or even 네 생일.

8.

앞으로는 자주 연락하고 지내요.

= From now on let us stay in touch more often.

9.

왜 그렇게 얼굴 보기가 힘들어요?

= Why is it so hard to meet you?

10.

오랜만에 만났는데 하나도 안 변했네요?

= It has been a long time and you have not changed a bit.

* Koreans also often say, "왜 안 늙어요?" which means, "Why aren't you aging?"

Track 37

11.

3년 전에 보고 처음 보는 거죠?

= This is the first time in three years we are seeing each other, right?

12.

옛날 그대로네요.

= You are exactly the same as before.

= You have not changed a bit.

* If it has not been a really long time, you can skip 옛날 and just say, "그대로네요."

Sample Dialogue

Track 38

예지: 어머, 혜진 씨, 오랜만이에요.

혜진: 예지 씨! 이게 얼마 만이에요. 잘 지냈어요?

예지: 네. 우리 3년 전에 보고 처음 보는 거죠?

혜진: 맞아요. 예지 씨 유학 가기 전에 보고 처음 보는 거잖아요.

예지: 너무 반가워요. 저 이제 한국 왔으니까 앞으로는 자주 연락하고 지내요!

Yeji: *Oh my, Hyejin, long time no see!*

Hyejin: *Yeji! It's been a long time. How have you been?*

Yeji: *Yeah, this is the first time in three years we're seeing each other, isn't it?*

Hyejin: *That's right. It's the first time we're seeing each other since you went to study abroad.*

Yeji: *It's so good to see you. Now that I'm in Korea, let's keep in touch more often!*

✏ Exercises for Lesson 19

Write the phrase that can fill in the two blanks.

1.

이게 ....이에요.

= It has been a long time.

............................에 보는 거죠?

= How long has it been since we last met?

Answer: ( )

2.

요새 어떻게 ....?

= How are you doing these days?

앞으로는 자주 연락하고 ....:

= Let us stay in touch more often from now on.

Answer: ( )

3.

3년 전에 보고 처음 ....?

= This is the first time in three years we are seeing each other, right?

얼마 만에 ....?

= How long has it been since we last met?

Answer: ( )

✎ Exercises for Lesson 19

4.

......................에 만났는데 하나도 안 변했네요?

= It has been a long time and you have not changed a bit.

......................이에요.

= Long time no see.

Answer: ( )

5.

3년 전에 .... 처음 보는 거죠?

= This is the first time in three years we are seeing each other, right?

작년 가을에 .... 못 봤죠?

= We have not seen each other since last fall, right?

Answer: ( )

Check the answers on **p. 218**

LESSON **20**

Sentence Building Drill 16

Sentence Building Drill 16

Track 39

In this series, we focus on how you can use the grammatical rules and expressions that you have learned previously to train yourself to comfortably make Korean sentences.

We will start off with THREE key sentences and practice changing different parts of these sentences, so that you do not end up simply memorizing the same three sentences. We want you to be able to make Korean sentences as flexibly as possible.

Key Sentence (1)

혼자 가면 심심할 테니까 제가 같이 간다니까요.

= I told you. I am going with you because it will be boring if you go alone.

Key Sentence (2)

제가 몸이 약해 보이지만, 사실은 아주 건강한 편이에요.

= I look weak, but in fact, I am quite healthy.

Key Sentence (3)

헬스장에 돈까지 낸 이상, 운동을 안 하면 아까울 테니까 열심히 하세요.

= Now that you have even paid for the gym, it will be a waste if you do not exercise, so work out hard.

Expansion & Variation Practice with Key Sentence (1)

0. Original Sentence:

혼자 가면 심심할 테니까 제가 같이 간다니까요.

= I told you. I am going with you because it will be boring if you go alone.

Track 39

1.

혼자 가면 심심할 테니까 = because it will be boring if you go alone

이대로 나가면 추울 테니까 = because it will be cold if you go out like this

너무 일찍 일어나면 피곤할 테니까 = because you will be tired if you get up too early

혼자 하면 힘들 테니까 = because it will be hard if you do it alone

2.

제가 같이 간다니까요. = I told you. I am going with you.

저 괜찮다니까요. = I told you. I am okay.

이게 제일 좋다니까요. = I told you. This is the best one.

혼자서도 할 수 있다니까요. = I told you. I can do this even by myself.

Expansion & Variation Practice with Key Sentence (2)

0. Original Sentence:

제가 몸이 약해 보이지만, 사실은 아주 건강한 편이에요.

= I look weak, but in fact, I am quite healthy.

1.

제가 몸이 약해 보이지만 = although I look weak

제가 어려 보이지만 = although I look very young

이게 처음에는 쉬워 보이지만 = although this looks easy at first

멀리서 보면 귀여워 보이지만 = although it looks cute from afar

2.

사실은 아주 건강한 편이에요. = I am actually pretty healthy.

친구들을 자주 만나는 편이에요. = I meet my friends quite often.

공부를 열심히 하는 편이에요. = I study pretty diligently.

저는 잠이 많은 편이에요. = I sleep quite a lot.

Track 39

Expansion & Variation Practice with Key Sentence (3)

0. Original Sentence:

헬스장에 돈까지 낸 이상, 운동을 안 하면 아까울 테니까 열심히 하세요.

= Now that you have even paid for the gym, it will be a waste if you do not exercise, so work out hard.

1.

헬스장에 돈까지 낸 이상 = now that you have even paid for the gym

* People in Korea often call gyms and fitness centers 헬스장, or sometimes even just 헬스.

사람들이 다 안 이상 = now that everybody has already found out

한국까지 온 이상 = since you have already come all the way to Korea

마음먹은 이상 = since you have already made up your mind

2.

운동을 안 하면 아까울 테니까 열심히 하세요.

= It will be a waste if you do not exercise, so work out hard.

너무 많이 넣으면 매울 테니 조금만 넣으세요.

= It will be spicy if you put in too much of it, so just add a little bit.

* Note that you can shorten 테니까 to 테니.

지금 가면 차가 막힐 테니 나중에 가세요.

= The traffic will be bad if you leave now, so go later.

내일 오면 저는 여기에 없을 테니 지금 이야기하세요.

= I will not be here if you come back tomorrow, so tell me now.

Track 39

Sample Dialogue

우현: 진혁 씨, 운동 좋아해요?

진혁: 네, 제가 운동 안 좋아할 것 같아 보이지만 굉장히 좋아하고 자주 하는 편이에요.

우현: 의외네요. 일주일에 운동 한 번 하는 거 아니에요?

진혁: 자주 한다니까요. 적어도 일주일에 세 번은 해요.

Woohyeon: Jinhyuk, do you enjoy exercising?

Jinhyuk: Yes. I look like I wouldn't enjoy exercising, but I really like it and I exercise pretty often.

Woohyun: That's surprising. It's not that you're just doing it once a week?

Jinhyuk: I'm telling you I do it often. I exercise at least three times a week.

✐ Exercises for Lesson 20

Translate each phrase or sentence into Korean and write it on the lines provided.

1. since you have already come all the way to Korea

....

2. because it will be hard if you do it alone

....

3. I told you. I can do this even by myself.

....

4. I am actually pretty healthy.

....

Check the answers on **p. 218**

5. The traffic will be bad if you leave now, so go later.

....

Through Idiomatic Phrases and More Advanced Grammar Points

BLOG

Yongsan Video Game Alley
(용산전자상가)

I do not know about you, but I am a huge fan of games. Since I was a kid, I have played video games. I cannot even remember how and when we first got a Nintendo because as far as I know, we had it before I was born, or at least before my first memory. But the first console game I do remember getting was the Super Nintendo. I even remember opening the package and starting it up. I would play it all the time. My favorite game to play on it was Super Mario World, and it is the first game I remember playing over and over. I beat it many times throughout the years.

As I got older, I got other game consoles (게임기) and continued my love for video games. When I moved to Korea, I was not able to bring any of my systems with me. At first, I was not sure how long I would be here or if I would even want to play games. I knew I would be doing a ton of exploring since it was a new place. However, as the years passed, I felt the itch to play games. I especially wanted to play some of the more classic game consoles like the NES or SNES. But was there even a place to buy such things in Korea? In the US, it is pretty easy to find older systems, but I wondered how easy it would be to buy them here in Korea.

Before we get into that though, let us look at a bit of the history of gaming in Korea. Those

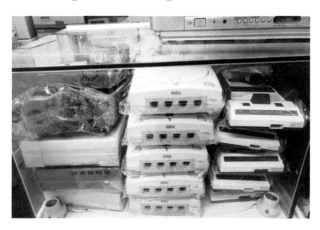

that know brands like SEGA or Nintendo, know just how popular they were back in the '80s and '90s. However, that was not the case here in Korea. In fact, these companies had a hard time releasing products in Korea so they licensed their console games to companies like Samsung and Hyundai. The names of the consoles were changed and the NES console version that Hyundai released did not come with any translated games. They were very popular—at one point, it was said there was a console in one out of every four homes in South Korea.

So, there is a base for these console games here in Korea and there are a few places you can visit to get your retro gaming fix. Of course, you can check out franchises like E-Mart or Toys R Us to find newer game systems, but if you are looking for something a bit older, here are a couple of places you can try visiting.

Yongsan Game Alley

One place you can go is the Yongsan Game Alley, located just outside of Yongsan Station. There you will find stack after stack of retro game consoles. I am not joking. I walked in and was quite surprised to see PlayStation, Dreamcast, Nintendo, and all sorts of other systems stacked on top of each other. If you are a collector, you can even find some rare Nintendo systems where the system and the game console are connected. And if you do not see anything that looks like the Nintendo you are familiar with, that is because they looked a bit

different and had a different name in Korea. For instance, the Super Nintendo was called the Super Famicom. Even if you are not going to play it, it would make for a great display as it looks slightly different than the US-version of the Super Nintendo.

As you walk down this alley of game after game, the shopkeepers will ask if you are looking for anything. If you are not sure what you are looking for, you can just say, "그냥 구경하는 거예요" or "그냥 둘러보는 거예요 (I am just browsing)." They tend to leave you alone after that and will talk to the other customers. If you want to know the price of something, you can say, "저기요. 이거 얼마예요? (Excuse me, how much is this?)" They will then give you the price.

Now, with these kinds of places, it is best to know how much you want to spend on something before going. I am not sure if they will lower their price or not, but if you are good at haggling, it is worth a shot. I am terrible at haggling, though, so if someone names a price more than I want to spend, I just say, "Okay", and move on without buying it. Which is what I did a lot of there. I knew beforehand how much some of the things cost, so once they told me it was more than that, I just moved on to admiring the other collections that stood before me. Although, I might have to go back to pick up some of the old GameBoys they had in stock as they looked really cool and were a decent price.

Nambu Terminal

There is another place you can visit as well if you are looking for both new and old gaming systems. It is near Nambu Bus Terminal and is called Kukje Electronics Center. Most of the gaming items are on the 9th floor, and there is plenty to look through.

They sell not only gaming consoles but also have all sorts of anime toys and collectibles as well. So, if you are looking to pick up some games as well as some collectibles, this might be the stop for you. One thing I noticed as well was that the people here seemed a bit friendlier than at Yongsan Game Alley. The prices here seemed to be a bit more fair as well so that is something to keep in mind when visiting. If you have the time, I suggest checking both places out to make sure you get the best price for the item you are looking for.

Since I do not live in Seoul, I cannot wait until my next trip back so I have an excuse to visit these places again and hopefully come away with some cool new toys. Who knows, maybe I can pick up a little gift for my nieces and nephews so they can play the games I grew up with.

Written by Johnny Bland

우와!

벌써 Lesson 20까지 공부했네요!
다음 레슨에는 어떤 재미있는 표현이 기다리고 있을까요?

LESSON 21

Advanced Idiomatic Expressions 10

생각 (Thought, Idea)

Track 41

This is an Advanced Idiomatic Expressions lesson related to 생각, "thought" or "idea". In order to fully understand and use the expressions introduced in this series, it is essential that you understand the grammatical structure of the sentences. When you come across a grammar point that you are unfamiliar with, please go back and review the related TTMIK lessons.

Keyword: **생각** = thought, idea

1. **생각이 다르다** = to have a different opinion
   ▷ **다르다** = to be different

Literally translated, it means "the thought is different", but the actual meaning of 생각이 다르다 is to have a different opinion from another person.

Ex)

저는 그 문제에 대해서는 생각이 좀* 달라요.

= About that matter, I have a slightly different opinion.

* A lot of people use 좀 to be tactful or to avoid sounding too strong. However, if someone uses 조금 rather than 좀, as in, "조금 달라요", they probably have a very different opinion.

2. 생각이 없다 = to not feel like eating/drinking

Literally translated 생각이 없다 means that you have no idea, or that you have not thought much about something. However, it is actually used to mean that you are not hungry or thirsty so you do not feel like eating or drinking. This phrase can also have a negative meaning, implying that someone is careless.

Track 41

Ex)

저는 아침을 늦게 먹어서 점심 생각이 없어요.

= I had a late breakfast, so I do not feel like having lunch (now).

3. 생각에 잠기다 = to be lost in thought

잠기다 literally means "to be submerged" or "to be flooded", so if you say that you are "flooded" by thoughts or are submerged in your thoughts, it means that you are deep in thought about something.

Ex)

무슨 생각에 잠겨 있었길래 전화 온 줄도 몰랐어요?

= What were you thinking about so hard? You did not even know that your phone was ringing.

147

4. 생각만 해도 = at the bare thought of it

The meaning of this one is fairly easy to guess, since it is translated as "even if I just think about it". This is most commonly used when talking about something that you are scared about, something you do not enjoy experiencing, or when someone mentions something that is very absurd or is unlikely to happen.

Ex)

생각만 해도 소름이 끼쳐요.

= Just thinking about it alone gives me goosebumps.

생각만 해도 웃음이 나요.

= Just thinking about it makes me smile or laugh.

Track 41

5. 생각하기도 싫다 = to not even want to think about it

When there is something you are not looking forward to and want to avoid if possible, you can say 생각하기도 싫다. You can also change it to 생각하고 싶지도 않다 to mean the same thing.

Ex)

다시 대학생이 되는 건 생각하기도 싫어요.

= I do not even want to think about becoming a university student. / I hate the idea of becoming a university student.

현우 씨가 여기에 온다고요? 생각하기도 싫어요.

= I hate the idea of Hyunwoo coming here.

* In this situation, you hate the thought of the person coming here. But if they are actually coming, you would not say this. You would just say, "싫어요."

6. 생각이 나다 = for a thought to occur, to remember

생각이 나다 can be used in two types of situations: when you just remembered something that you previously could not recall (like someone's name or the reason you called someone), or when something just occurred to you and you started thinking about it. When you are just going about your daily tasks and all of a sudden you think of someone that you know, you can say 생각이 나다. This phrase can also be written as one word, 생각나다.

Ex)

그냥 네 생각 나서 전화했어.

= I just thought of you, so I am calling you now.

생각(이) 나면 말해 주세요.

= Let me know if you think of it.

Track
41

7. 생각이 들다 = for a thought to occur

생각이 들다 and 생각이 나다 are similar in usage, but 생각이 들다 is used only when talking about the actual "content" of a thought. You can say 생각이 나다 when a person or place comes to mind, and you can use 생각이 들다 to talk about an opinion or premonition. In many cases, 생각이 들다 is just translated as "to think", "to feel", or "to have a feeling".

Ex)

이거 조금 이상하다는 생각 안 들어요?

= Don't you feel that this is a bit strange?

8. -(으)ㄹ 생각은 없다 = to not intend to do something

When you feel bad about something you have said or done and want to apologize, one expression that can come in handy is -(으)ㄹ 생각은 없다. If you just say 생각 없다, it can either mean "to be not very hungry" or "to be thoughtless or careless", but if you use -(으)ㄹ 생각은 없다 with a specific verb stem, it means that you do not intend to do something.

Ex)

놀라게 할 생각은 없었어요.

= I did not intend to surprise you.

겁줄 생각은 없었어요.

= I did not intend to scare you.

Track 41

9. 생각이 간절하다 = to really want to have (usually a certain food/drink)

간절하다 means "ardent" or "desperate", so if you say 생각이 간절하다, it means that you have a very strong yearning for something, usually a certain food or drink.

Ex)

요즘에 다이어트 하고 있는데, 운동하고 나면 콜라 생각이 간절해요.

= I am on a diet these days, and after I work out, I really want a Coke.

지금 물 생각이 간절하다.

= I really want some water right now.

10. 생각지도 못했던 일이다 = to be unthought-of, to have not been foreseen

생각지도 is short for 생각하지도, and by saying that something was 생각지도 못했던 일, you are saying that you did not have the faintest idea that something like that could happen.

Ex)

이건 정말 생각지도 못했던 결과네요.

= We really did not see this coming.

= This is really an unexpected result.

II. 생각해 보고 말 것도 없다 = to not even be worth thinking about

Here, 말다 means "to not do something", and this usage of 말다 is always used in the form of -아/어/여 보고 말 것도 없다, which means that something "is not even worth trying to do". Literally it means "there is not enough (substance or importance to it) to really bother doing it".

Track 41

Ex)

생각해 보고 말 것도 없이, 그 사람은 무조건 안 돼요.

= It is not even worth thinking about, he just cannot do it.

= Needless to say, my answer is no. I cannot let him do it.

12. -을/를 생각해서라도 = at least for the sake of (someone)

Literally translated, this means "even if you were to do it, just think about (someone else)". In actual usage, it means "at least for the sake of (someone)". This is commonly used when you want to persuade someone to do something that they do not want to do.

Ex)

가기 싫겠지만, 나를 생각해서라도 한 번만 참석해 줘.

= I know you do not want to go, but please attend just this once, at least for me.

* You might hear people say 부모님을 생각해서라도 to say, "at least do it for your parents".

Sample Dialogue

Track
42

지우: 나는 고등학교 시절 생각만 해도 기분이
　　　좋아져.

현진: 진짜? 나는 고등학교 시절은
　　　생각하기도 싫은데.

지우: 그래? 그럼 너는 고등학교 선생님 되고
　　　싶은 생각은 없겠네.

현진: 응, 전혀 생각 없지.

*Jiwoo: Just thinking about when I was in high
　　　school, I feel happier.*

*Hyunjin: Really? I don't like to even think about my
　　　high school days.*

*Jiwoo: Is that so? Then you must never want to be
　　　a high school teacher.*

Hyunjin: Nope. Never.

✏ Exercises for Lesson 21

Fill in the blanks with the appropriate idioms with 생각 *from this lesson.*

1. (   )

= for a thought to occur, to remember

2. (   )

= to not feel like eating/drinking

3. (   )

= to really want to have (usually a certain food/drink)

4. (   )

= to not even want to think about it

5. (   )

= to be lost in thought

Check the answers on **p. 218**

LESSON **22**

Word Builder 20

시(示, 視)

Word Builder lessons are designed to help you understand how to expand your vocabulary by learning and understanding some common and basic building blocks of Korean words. The words and letters introduced through Word Builder lessons are not necessarily all Chinese characters, or 한자, and although many of them are based on Chinese characters, their meanings can differ from modern-day Chinese. Your goal, through these lessons, is to understand how Korean words are formed and remember keywords in Korean to expand your Korean vocabulary from there. You certainly don't have to memorize the Hanja characters, but if you want to, feel free!

Today's key word element is 시.

We are introducing two Chinese characters for this lesson: 示 and 視. The first one, 示 means "to show", and the second one, 視 means "to see".

示

시 (show) + 범 (good example) = 시범 示範 = demonstration

Related Vocabulary

모범 模範 = good example

태권도 시범 跆拳道 示範 = taekwondo demonstration

시범 경기 示範 競技 = exhibition match, demonstration match

시범 수업 示範 授業 = demonstration class

예 (example) + 시 (show) = 예시 例示 = example, illustration

Related Vocabulary

예를 들어서 = for example

과 (boast) + 시 (show) = 과시 誇示 = showing off

게 (put up, post) + 시 (show) = 게시 揭示 = put up, post

Related Vocabulary

게시하다 揭示-- = to put up, to post

게시되다 揭示-- = to be posted

게시물 揭示物 = written posts

게시판 揭示板 = bulletin board

표 (outside, surface) + 시 (show) = 표시 表示 = expression or show (of emotion)

Related Vocabulary

표면 表面 = surface

감정 표시 感情 表示 = show of emotion

표 (mark) + 시 (show) = 표시 標示 = mark, sign

Related Vocabulary

가격 표시 **價格 標示** = price mark

Note the difference in the Hanja characters between the two 표시s. In real life, since the meanings are related, unless asked to pay attention to the Hanja, most people will regard them as exactly the same word.

Track 43

시 (see) + 력 (power) = 시력 視力 = eyesight, vision

시 (see) + 청 (listen) = 시청 視聽 = watching and listening

Related Vocabulary

시청하다 視聽 – – = to watch and listen

시청자 視聽者 = viewer, audience

시청각 자료 視聽覺 資料 = audio, video material

시 (see) + 각 (realize) = 시각 視覺 = sight, vision

* 각(覺) is often used with one's senses.

Related Vocabulary

시각적인 視覺的– = visual

시각 디자인 視覺 ––– = visual design

감각 感覺 = sense

청각 聽覺 = sense of hearing

촉각 觸覺 = sense of touch

시 (see) + 야 (field) = 시야 視野 = one's view, field of vision

Ex)

시야가 넓다 視野––– = one's view is wide

시야가 좁다 視野––– = one's view is narrow

시야가 확보되다 視野– 確保–– = visibility is established, to secure a clear view

Track
43

Related Vocabulary

야구 野球 = baseball; the literal translation is "field ball"

시 (see) + 찰 (examine) = 시찰 視察 = inspection

* You will often see this word in political news.

시 (see) + 선 (line) = 시선 視線 = attention, gaze

Ex)

사람들의 시선이 부담스러워요. = I feel so pressured by other people's attention.

시선을 어디에 두어야 할지 모르겠어요. = I don't know where to look.

시선 처리 視線 處理 = the direction of one's gaze or where one's eyes are directed

Sample Dialogue

Track
44

예지: 박주연 선생님, 이번 시범 수업 때 어떤
시청각 자료 쓰실 거예요?

주연: 아! 게시판에 올려서 공유할게요.

예지: 아, 언제 올리실 거예요?

주연: 오늘 밤에 올릴게요.

*Yeji: Mrs. Park, what audiovisual materials will you
use for the demonstration this time?*

*Jooyeon: Ah! I will upload and share them on the
online bulletin board.*

Yeji: Oh, when will you upload them?

Jooyeon: I'll upload them tonight.

✏ Exercises for Lesson 22

1. What is the difference in meaning between the two Chinese characters, 示 and 視?

....

Fill in the blanks with the appropriate Sino-Korean word from the lesson.

2. (   )   =   sight, vision

3. (   )   =   eyesight, vision

4. (   )   =   attention, gaze

5. (   )   =   example, illustration

6. Among the four words above, which word consists of 시(示)?

....

LESSON **23**

While

-(으)면서

Track 45

The structure -(으)면서 can be translated into English as "while", and similar to the way "while" is used in English, -(으)면서 has a few different usages in Korean depending on the context.

Usages of -(으)면서

I.

You can use -(으)면서 to describe how you are engaging in two actions at the same time, or how you do one thing while also doing another thing, such as "studying Korean while cleaning the house" or "exercising while listening to music".

> *Conjugation*
> Verb stem + -(으)면서

Ex)

공부하다 + -(으)면서 + 운동하다 = 공부하면서 운동해요. (= I exercise while studying.)

Sample Sentences

저는 샤워하면서 노래를 들어요.

= I listen to music while taking a shower.

저는 샤워하면서 노래를 불러요.

= I sing while taking a shower.

저는 잠을 자면서 많이 움직여요.

= I move my body a lot while sleeping.

Track 45

저는 학교에 다니면서 아르바이트를 많이 했어요.

= I did a lot of part-time work while going to school.

* This example refers to attending school, rather than literally traveling to school.

저는 노래를 들으면서 일을 할 수가 없어요.

= I cannot work while listening to music.

운전하면서 전화 통화 하지 마세요.

= Do not talk on the phone while driving.

2.

You can also contrast two actions or states by linking them with -(으)면서. When one state or action betrays or is the opposite of the other action, you can use -(으)면서 between the two verbs.

162

Ex)

알면서 모르는 척했어요?

= You knew but pretended you did not know?

Sample Sentences

좋으면서 관심 없는 척하지 마세요.

= Do not pretend you are uninterested when you are excited.

알지도 못하면서 쉽게 말하지 마세요.

= You do not know (it/him/them/me) well, so do not speak about it so casually.

준비는 하면서도* 걱정이 됐어요.

= Even as I was preparing for it and everything, I was worried.

* -도 here is adding more emphasis to the fact that you were worried.

Track 45

3.

You can use the -(으)면서 structure with action verbs, as well as with nouns and the -이다 verb, in which case the structure changes to "noun + -(이)면서". To express the future tense, you use -(으)ㄹ 것 + -이면서, which is shortened to -(으)ㄹ 거면서. This is because the future tense in Korean is basically "verb stem + -(으)ㄹ 것이다", which uses the -이다 verb already.

Ex)

학생이면서 동시에 모델이에요.

= She is a student and model at the same time.

* This can also be expressed by saying "학생이기도 하면서 동시에 모델이에요."

결국에 올 거면서 어제는 왜 그렇게 말했어요?

= You were going to come here anyway, so why did you say that (you would not) yesterday?

Sample Sentences

그 사람은 제 친구이면서 동시에 선생님이에요.

= She is both my friend and my teacher.

시간 없다고 할 거면서...

= I know you are going to say you do not have time (and yet you are not saying so).

하지도 못할 거면서 큰소리치지 마세요.

= Do not bluff about it while (it is obvious that) you are not going to be able to do it anyway.

Track 45

Sample Dialogue

Track 46

신애: 해리 씨는 하는 일도 많으면서 드라마는 도대체 언제 봐요?

해리: 퇴근하고 집에 가면서 봐요.

신애: 아, 지하철에서요?

해리: 네. 드라마 보면 시간이 금방 가서 좋더라고요.

Shinae: When on earth do you watch dramas when you have so much work?

Harry: I watch them on my way home after work.

Shinae: Oh, on the subway?

Harry: Yes. It's nice because time passes quickly when I watch dramas.

✏️ Exercises for Lesson 23

Translate each sentence into Korean using –(으)면서 *or* –(이)면서 *and write it down on the lines provided.*

1. I sing while taking a shower.

....

2. I move my body a lot while sleeping.

....

3. I did a lot of part-time work while going to school.

....

Check the answers on **p. 218**

4. You do not know (it/him/them/me) well, so do not speak about it so casually.

....

5. She is both my friend and my teacher.

....

166

LESSON **24**

Didn't you say…?, I heard that…

-(ㄴ/는)다면서요, -(이)라면서요

If you are familiar with the structure -(으)면서, which was introduced in the previous lesson, it is easy to guess what -(ㄴ/는)다면서요 and -(이)라면서요 mean. However, if you try to translate sentences using -(ㄴ/는)다면서요 and -(이)라면서요 literally to English, the translations are very different from the actual meanings of the sentences because -(ㄴ/는) 다면서요 and -(이)라면서요 are used as sentence endings.

Origins

-(ㄴ/는)다면서(요) is a combination of -(ㄴ/는)다 and -다고 말하면서, and the literal translation is "saying ABC while doing XYZ". Similarly, -(이)라면서(요) is originally -(이)다 + -라고 말하면서 and, therefore literally translates to "while saying that ABC is XYZ".

However, when used to end a sentence, -(ㄴ/는)다면서(요) and -(이)라면서(요) have a different meaning than when they are used in the middle of a sentence. Note that the endings have -요 at the end for 존댓말.

Actual Usage

-(ㄴ/는)다면서요 and -(이)라면서요 can be used when you want to show your surprise or dissatisfaction after finding out that what you thought was true is not, or when you are fact-checking what you heard before from someone else.

Ex)

집에 가다 + -ㄴ다면서요 = 집에 간다면서요 = you said you were going home (but you are here)

학생 + -이라면서요 = 학생이라면서요 = you said you were a student (yet, apparently, you are not)

There is also another usage that uses the imperative.

Track
47

Ex)

가다 + -라면서요 = 가라면서요 = you told me to leave (and now you are saying otherwise)

오지 말다 + -라면서요 = 오지 말라면서요 = you told me not to come

Also, for example, if someone gives you a slice of cake and tells you to eat it, and then later gets hungry and asks where the cake is, you can reply, "먹으라면서요! (= You told me to eat it!)" Please note that even though they told you to eat it in the past, you do not use this imperative sentence in the past tense.

These endings do not always turn the sentence into a question, but it is very common to put a question mark at the end of the sentence to emphasize the fact that the speaker is surprised, disappointed, or intrigued, depending on the context.

Sample Sentences

다음 달에 이사 간다면서요?

= I heard you are going to move next month.

벌써 다 끝났다면서요?

= I heard it is already over. Is that right?

아직 학생이라면서요!

= Didn't you say you are still a student?

잘 모르는 사이라면서요!

= You said you did not know each other that well!

형이 의사라면서요?

= I heard your older brother is a doctor.

Please note that the meanings of theses can vary depending on your intonation.

Sample Dialogue

Track 48

경은: 예지 씨, 다음 달에 이사 간다면서요?

예지: 네, 회사 근처로 이사 가요.

경은: 네? 아직 학생이라면서요!

예지: 아, 아직 학교 졸업 안 했는데,
　　　취업했어요. 다음 달부터 출근해요.

*Kyeong-eun: Yeji, I heard you are going to move
　　　next month.*

Yeji: Yes. I'm moving close to my office.

Kyeong-eun: What? You said you're still a student!

*Yeji: Ah, I haven't graduated from school yet, but I
　　　got a job. I start work next month.*

✏ *Exercises for Lesson* **24**

Translate each sentence into Korean using **-(ㄴ/는)다면서요** *or* **-(이)라면서요** *and then write it on the lines provided below.*

1. I heard you are going to move next month.

....

2. I heard it is already over. Is that right?

....

3. Didn't you say you are still a student?

....

4. You said you did not know each other that well!

....

5. I heard your older brother is a doctor.

....

Check the answers on **p. 219**

LESSON 25

Advanced Situational Expressions 12

길을 물어볼 때
(When You Ask For Directions)

Track 49

Welcome to another lesson in the Advanced Situational Expressions series. Throughout this series, we go over common situations and some of the advanced Korean expressions you can use in each of them. In this lesson, we will introduce various expressions you can use when you are asking for or giving directions.

1.

저기요, 죄송하지만 길 좀 물을게요.

= Excuse me, I am sorry, but I would like to ask for directions.

* You can end this sentence in many different ways, such as 물을게요, 물어볼게요, 묻고 싶은데요, etc.

** If you just say "길 좀 물을게요" without saying 저기요, 죄송하지만 first, it is too sudden and people might be put off. Saying 저기요, 죄송하지만 first prepares them to listen to you.

2.

혹시 길 좀 물을 수 있을까요?

= By any chance, could I ask you for directions?

172

3.

서울역이 어느 쪽이에요?

= Which way is Seoul Station?

* You could also say, "서울역이 이쪽이에요, 저쪽이에요? (= Is Seoul Station this way or that way?)"

** Of course, you can replace 서울역 with any other place name.

4.

교보문고 가려면* 어디로 가야 돼요?

= Where should I go if I want to get to Kyobo Bookstore?

* 가려면 = in order to go, if I want to go

5.

어린이대공원으로 가려면 어느 쪽으로 가야 돼요?

= Which way should I go to get to Children's Grand Park?

6.

서울대학교 정문이 어디예요?

= Where is the main gate of Seoul National University?

* 정문 = main gate / 입구 = entrance / 후문 = back gate

7.

현대백화점이 어딘지* 아세요?

= Do you know where Hyundai Department Store is?

* 어딘지 is short for 어디인지.

8.

이 근처에 하나은행이 어디에 있는지 아세요?

= Do you know where a Hana Bank is around here?

173

9.

저도 잘 모르겠네요.

= I do not know either.

* If you just say "몰라요", it sounds a bit rude, so it's better to say "모르겠어요", "모르겠네요", or "모르겠는데요."

10.

저도 여기 사람이 아니라서 잘 모르겠네요.

= I am not from around here either, so I do not know.

* You can also say "저도 오늘 처음 왔어요. (= It is my first time here, too.)"

11.

하나은행이요? 모르겠어요.

= Hana Bank? I do not know.

* By repeating the name of the place, you are showing that you are trying to help.

Track 49

12.

이쪽으로 가셔서 다시 한 번 물어보세요.

= Go this way and ask someone one more time.

* You can replace 이쪽으로 with other expressions, such as 저쪽으로, 저기로, etc., that fit the situation.

13.

이쪽으로 100미터 정도 가셔서 왼쪽으로 가면 있어요.

= If you go 100 meters this way and turn left, it will be there.

14.

여기서 걸어가기에는 거리가 좀 있어요. 버스 타셔야 될 거예요.

= It is a bit of a distance to walk from here. You will need to take a bus.

* **거리가 좀 있어요.** = It is a bit of a walk. / It is a bit of a distance to walk.

Sample Dialogue

Track 50

민수: 저기요, 죄송하지만 길 좀 물을게요.
　　　서울역이 어느 쪽이에요?

행인1: 저도 잘 모르겠네요.

민수: 저기 죄송한데, 혹시 길 좀 물을 수
　　　있을까요? 서울역이 어느 쪽이에요?

행인2: 이쪽으로 쭉 가시면 되는데,
　　　걸어가기에는 거리가 좀 있어요. 버스
　　　타셔야 될 거예요.

민수: 네, 감사합니다.

*Minsu: Excuse me, I'm sorry, but I need directions.
Which way is Seoul Station?*

Passerby 1: I'm not sure, either.

*Minsu: I'm sorry, can I ask you for directions?
Which way is Seoul Station?*

*Passerby 2: You can go straight this way, but it's a
bit far to walk. You will need to take a bus.*

Minsu: Okay, thank you.

✎ Exercises for Lesson 25

Write the phrase that can fill in the two blanks.

1.

저기요, 죄송하지만 ....게요.

= Excuse me, I am sorry, but I would like to ask for directions.

혹시 .... 수 있을까요?

= By any chance, could I ask you for directions?

Answer: (   )

2.

서울역이 .... 이에요?

= Which way is Seoul Station?

어린이대공원으로 가려면 .... 으로 가야 돼요?

= Which way should I go to get to Children's Grand Park?

Answer: (   )

3.

현대백화점이 어딘지 ....?

= Do you know where Hyundai Department Store is?

이 근처에 하나은행이 어디에 있는지 ....?

= Do you know where a Hana Bank is around here?

Answer: (   )

4.

저도 ....

= I do not know either.

저도 여기 사람이 아니라서 ....

= I am not from around here either, so I do not know.

Answer: (   )

5.

.... 가셔서 다시 한 번 물어보세요.

= Go this way and ask someone one more time.

.... 100미터 정도 가셔서 왼쪽으로 가면 있어요.

= If you go 100 meters this way and turn left, it will be there.

Answer: (   )

Check the answers on **p. 219**

LESSON **26**

Advanced Idiomatic Expressions 11

시간 (Time)

Track
51

In this Advanced Idiomatic Expressions lesson, we give you 12 phrases related to 시간 (time) that you can use when you want to say "I do not have time", "stop wasting time", "do you have enough time?" and so on. The sentences in this series do not have an exact word-by-word breakdown, but they do have an English translation. You can memorize these sentences and/or break them down on your own to review vocabulary and sentence structures. However, you choose to learn, make sure you come back and study with us every day! Have fun!

Keyword: 시간 = time

1. **시간을 내다** = to make time for something/someone

   Ex)
   잠깐 시간 좀 내 줄 수 있어요?
   = Can you make some time for me?

2. **이러고 있을 시간이 없다** = to not have time for this

▷ 이러고 있다 is short for 이렇게 하고 있다 (= to be doing this, to be doing it like this)

▷ -(으)ㄹ 시간 = time for something, time to do something

Ex)

지금 이러고 있을 시간이 없어요.

= You do not have time for this.

우리 지금 이러고 있을 시간이 없어요.

= We do not have time for this.

지금 이러고 있을 시간이 어디 있어요?

= You do not have time for this. (lit. Where is the time for doing this?)

3. **그럴 시간 있으면** = if you have that kind of time

▷ 그럴 시간 = time for doing such a thing, that kind of time

Ex)

그럴 시간 있으면 공부나 하세요.

= If you have that kind of time, just study.

* This is what teachers or parents usually say to their students or children when they are not studying. Sometimes, parents also say this with the meaning of, "You did not have to do that" when they receive a gift from their children.

4. **시간을 할애하다** = to spare some time

▷ 할애하다 = (formal) to spend, to spare

Ex)

이번 프로젝트에 시간을 많이 할애해 주세요.

179

= Please spend a lot of time on this project.

5. 한국 시간으로 = in Korean local time

If you want to say the time in a certain time zone, you can just say the country or city name and then 시간. For example, "뉴욕 시간으로 (= in New York local time)", "일본 시간으로 (= in Japanese local time)", etc.

Ex)
한국 시간으로 5월 2일 오후 7시에 시작할 거예요.
= It will begin at 7 p.m. on May 2nd in Korean local time.

Track
51

6. 좀처럼 시간이 안 나다 = just cannot find the time

▷ 좀처럼 adds the nuance of, "I really tried, but I just cannot seem to do it."

Ex)
여행을 가고 싶은데 좀처럼 시간이 안 나네요.
= I want to travel, but I just cannot find the time.

7. 시간을 낭비하다 = to waste time

Ex)
괜히 시간 낭비하지 말고 그냥 돌아가세요.
= Stop wasting your time and just go back home.
* 괜히 = for nothing, in vain

8. **시간이 남아돌다** = to have some spare time lying around

  ▷ **남다** = to remain, to be left

  ▷ **남아돌다** = to be more than enough, to be in excess

  Ex)

  제가 시간이 남아도는 줄 아세요?

  = Do you think I have that much time to waste?

9. **-(으)ㄹ 시간도 없다** = to not even have time for

  Ex)

  아무리 바빠도 그렇죠. 잠깐 전화할 시간도 없어요?

  = Even though you were really busy, you did not even have time for a quick phone call?

  아무리 바빠도 그렇죠. 청소할 시간도 없어요?

  = Even though you were really busy, you did not even have time to clean?

  아무리 바빠도 그렇지. 잠깐 저녁 먹을 시간도 없어?

  = Even though you were really busy, you did not even have time for a quick dinner?

Track 51

10. **시간이 가다** = time passes, time goes by

  Ex)

  시간이 어떻게 가는지 모르겠어요.

  = I cannot feel the passage of time.

  = Time flies.

11. **시간을 되돌리다** = to turn back time

▷ **돌리다** = to turn something

▷ **되-** = back (to the original)

▷ **되돌리다** = to turn it back

Ex)

시간을 되돌릴 수 있으면 좋겠어요.

= I wish I could turn back time to the past.

12. **시간을 보내다** = to spend time doing something

Track 51

Ex)

저는 주말에는 가족들하고 시간을 보내요.

= I spend time with my family on the weekends.

Sample Dialogue

주연: 저희 호주 다녀온 게 벌써 3년
      전이에요.

경은: 벌써 그렇게 지났어요? 우와, 시간이
      어떻게 가는지 모르겠네요.

주연: 시간을 되돌릴 수 있으면 좋겠어요.
      호주 진짜 좋았는데...

경은: 저도 호주로 또 여행 가고 싶은데
      좀처럼 시간이 안 나네요.

*Jooyeon: It's already been three years since we
      went to Australia.*

*Kyeong-eun: Has it already been that long? Wow,
      time sure flies.*

*Jooyeon: I wish I could turn back time. Australia
      was so nice...*

*Kyeong-eun: I want to go on vacation to Australia
      again too, but I just can't find the time.*

✏️ Exercises for Lesson **26**

Fill in the blanks with the appropriate idioms with 시간 *from the lesson.*

1. ( )

   = to have some spare time lying around

2. ( )

   = to make time for something/someone

3. ( )

   = to turn back time

4. ( )

   = to spare some time

5. ( )

   = in Korean local time

Check the answers on **p. 219**

LESSON **27**

And now, But now

-더니

It is time to learn another very cool grammar point that will help you enrich your Korean conversations! In this lesson, we are looking at the verb ending -더니. In general, you can use -더니 when you are describing what happened in relation to your discovery of a fact.

Track
53

Usages of -더니

I.

You can use -더니 when you describe two things that you experienced or observed, one after the other. The two things that happened can be either the opposite of each other, very different from each other (therefore surprising you), or just connected to each other in sequence. Therefore, depending on the context, the English translation of -더니 can be very different. Note that you cannot really use this phrase in the future tense.

Sample Sentences

어제는 비가 오더니 오늘은 눈이 오네요.

= It rained yesterday, but it is snowing today.

예지 씨가 어제는 9시에 오더니, 오늘은 11시에 왔어요.

= Yeji came in at 9 o'clock yesterday, and she came in at 11 o'clock today.

   * You are simply emphasizing the difference between the two times by using -더니, not implying that one is better or worse than the other.

경화 씨가 어제는 요가를 하더니, 오늘은 테니스를 하네요.

= Kyung-hwa did yoga yesterday, and today she is playing tennis.

   * By using -더니, you are implying that you find it interesting to see Kyung-hwa do different sports every day.

아침에는 춥더니 지금은 따뜻하네요.

= It was cold in the morning, but now it is warm.

Track 53

제 컴퓨터가 느려지더니, 이제 안 켜져요.

= My computer slowed down, and now it will not even switch on.

   * In this case, you are not comparing two different things. Instead, you are describing two things that happened one after another in a time sequence.

두 사람이 커피숍 앞에서 만나더니 뭔가 물건을 교환했어요.

= Those two people met in front of a coffee shop, and then exchanged something with each other.

석진 씨가 밖에 나가더니 갑자기 고양이를 데리고 왔어요.

= Seokjin went outside, and then suddenly, he brought back a cat.

   * Again, remember that you have to have seen something with your own eyes to be able to use -더니. If you did not see either of the two actions, you cannot use -더니.

2.

The second usage is similar to the first, but in this case, you can use -더니 when one thing is either a sign of the other (which is usually bigger, more intense, or more serious), or the direct result of it. In this case, if you are talking about something you did in the past, you need to add -았/었/였- between the verb stem and -더니. However, if you are talking about what someone else did in the past, just combine the verb stem and -더니, without using -았/었/였-.

Sample Sentences

책을 많이 읽었더니 눈이 피곤해요.

= I read a lot, so my eyes are tired.

도너츠를 많이 먹었더니 배탈이 났어요.

= I ate a lot of doughnuts, and now I have a stomachache.

Track 53

아침에 날씨가 흐리더니 오후에는 눈이 왔어요.

= The weather was overcast in the morning, and it ended up snowing in the afternoon.

석진 씨가 열심히 운동을 하더니 몸이 정말 좋아졌어요.

= Seokjin exercised hard, and now he has a really nice body.

경화 씨가 매일 글을 쓰더니 지난달에 소설을 출간했어요.

= Kyung-hwa wrote every day, and she published a novel last month.

* The previous action (writing every day) and the following action (publishing a novel) are related, but you are implying that you did not expect the following action to happen.

무거운 짐을 들고 왔더니 허리가 아파요.

= I carried some heavy luggage here, and because of that my back hurts.

187

* You can also say 와서 or 왔기 때문에 instead of 왔더니, but -더니 adds a bit more nuance that you did not know your back would hurt.

노래방에서 노래를 두 시간 동안 불렀더니 목소리가 안 나와요.

= I sang for two hours in a noraebang, and so I've lost my voice now.

    * 노래방 (noraebang) is a place where you rent a private room equipped with microphones, a video screen, and a selection of songs to sing.

노래방에 매일 다니더니 가수가 됐어요.

= He/she went to a noraebang every day, and he/she became a singer.

TalkToMeInKorean으로 매일 공부하더니 지금은 한국어를 잘해요.

= He/she studied through TalkToMeInKorean every day, and now he/she speaks Korean well.

Track 53

Sample Dialogue

Track
54

정민: 지은 씨, 어디 아파요?

지은: 아침에는 머리가 깨질 것 같이
　　　아프더니, 오후 되니까 온몸에 열이
　　　나네요.

정민: 몸살감기 아니에요? 저 감기약
　　　있는데, 줄까요?

지은: 아니에요. 괜찮아요. 아까 밥 먹고 약
　　　사 먹었더니 조금 나아지고 있는 것
　　　같아요.

Jeongmin: Jieun, are you sick?

*Jieun: In the morning my head hurt so bad it felt
like it was going to split open, and now that
it's the afternoon, my whole body is feverish.*

*Jeongmin: Isn't that the flu? I have some cold
medicine, should I give you some?*

*Jieun: No. It's okay. I ate earlier and took some
medicine so I think I'm getting a little better.*

✎ Exercises for Lesson **27**

These are the two usages of **-더니**. Read the sentences below and write which usage of **-더니** is used in the sentence.

A. You can use -더니 when you describe two things that you experienced or observed, one after the other. The two things that happened can be either the opposite of each other, very different from each other (therefore surprising you), or just connected to each other in sequence.

B. You can use -더니 when one thing is either a sign of the other (usually something bigger, more intense, or more serious), or the direct result of it.

Check the answers on **p. 219**

1. 경화 씨가 어제는 요가를 하더니, 오늘은 테니스를 하네요. (   )

2. 석진 씨가 열심히 운동을 하더니 몸이 정말 좋아졌어요. (   )

3. 책을 많이 읽었더니 눈이 피곤해요. (   )

4. 제 컴퓨터가 느려지더니, 이제 안 켜져요. (   )

5. 아침에는 춥더니 지금은 따뜻하네요. (   )

LESSON **28**

Rather than, Would rather

-(으)ㄹ 바에

In this TTMIK lesson, we will be introducing how -(으)ㄹ 바에 works and when you can use

it. Although this grammatical structure is fairly straightforward, the meaning of it is rather complex. To be able to use it, it is essential to understand what 바 means. 바 is a dependent noun that is rarely used on its own, but when paired with other verbs, 바 can mean "method", "content", or "situation". Used in -(으)ㄹ 바에, 바 means "situation" or "fact".

> ### Conjugation
>
> Verb stem + -(으)ㄹ 바에
> = Verb stem + -(으)ㄹ 바에야
> = Verb stem + -(으)ㄹ 바에는

When you link two actions with -(으)ㄹ 바에, you imply that the first action or option is much worse than the second action or option, or that the first option is so disappointing that you would rather choose the second.

191

Ex)

식은 라면을 먹다 = to eat ramyeon noodles that have become cold

안 먹다 = to not eat

→ 식은 라면을 먹을 바에는 그냥 안 먹을게요.

= If I have to eat ramyeon noodles that have gone cold, I would rather just not eat (at all).

Since you are saying that the second option (the action which comes after -(으)ㄹ 바에) is better than the first, you can also add expressions related to comparisons such as the following:

1. 차라리 = would rather

2. 낫다 = to be better

3. 그냥 = just

4. -고 말다 = to just do something and be done with the matter

Ex)

식은 라면을 먹을 바에는 차라리 그냥 안 먹고 말겠어요.

= If I have to eat ramyeon noodles that have gone cold, I would rather just not eat (at all).

식은 라면을 먹을 바에는 그냥 안 먹는 게 낫겠어요.

= If I have to eat ramyeon noodles that have gone cold, it would be better to just not eat (at all).

Sample Sentences

그 사람이랑 여행을 갈 바에는 저는 차라리 그냥 집에 있겠어요.

= If I have to go on a trip with him, I would rather just stay at home.

  * You are also implying that staying at home is not particularly enjoyable, but it is better than going with that person.

너랑 결혼할 바에야 평생 혼자 사는 게 낫지.

= If I have to marry you, it would be better to live by myself forever.

나중에 후회할 바에는 그냥 안 하는 게 낫겠어요.

= If you are going to regret it later, it would be better to just not do it.

이렇게 고민할 바에야 차라리 다른 사람한테 시키고 말겠어요.

= If this is going to be such a headache, I would rather just ask someone else to do it.

처음부터 다시 할 바에는 안 하는 게 낫겠어요.

= If we have to do it all over again, it would be better to not do it.

Exceptions

Since 바 has the meaning of "situation", -(으)ㄹ 바에 can also imply "if you are going to do it anyway". In this usage, it is usually preceded by 이왕 or 어차피. 이왕 is often translated as "already" or "now that", and 어차피 is often translated as "anyway" or "after all".

Sample Sentences

어차피 살 바에는 좋은 걸로 사세요.

= If you are going to buy one anyway, get a good one.

이왕 고칠 바에는 처음부터 다시 하는 게 낫겠어요.

= If you are going to modify it, it would be better to do it all over again.

어차피 잠깐밖에 못 쓸 바에는 중고로 사는 게 좋죠.

= If I will not be able to use it for long anyway, it is better to just buy it second hand.

Sample Dialogue

민영: 키가 작아서 무대가 안 보여요.

서준: 이쪽으로 와요. 거기 서서 힘들게 볼 바에는 아예 맨 뒤로 오는 게 낫지 않겠어요?

민영: 네? 거기서 볼 바에야 차라리 저기 좌석에 앉는 게 낫죠.

Minyoung: I'm so short that I can't see the stage.

Seojoon: Come this way. Wouldn't it be better to just come to the back with me rather than stand there where it's hard to see?

Minyoung: What? Rather than watching from over there where you are, I may as well go sit in a seat over there, in that area.

✏ Exercises for Lesson 28

Fill in the blanks to match the English translation.

1. 그 사람이랑 여행을 갈 바에는 저는 차라리 그냥 집에 ( ).

= If I have to go on a trip with him, I would rather just stay at home.

2. ( ) 살 바에는 좋은 걸로 사세요.

= If you are going to buy one anyway, get a good one.

3. 처음부터 다시 할 바에는 안 하는 게 ( ).

= If we have to do it all over again, it would be better to not do it.

4. 이렇게 고민할 바에야 ( ) 다른 사람한테 시키고 말겠어요.

= If this is going to be such a headache, I would rather just ask someone else to do it.

5. 어차피 잠깐밖에 못 쓸 ( ) 중고로 사는 게 좋죠.

= If I will not be able to use it for long anyway, it is better to just buy it second hand.

Check the answers on **p. 219**

195

LESSON **29**

Advanced Situational Expressions 13

차가 막힐 때
(When The Traffic Is Bad)

Track
57

Almost nobody enjoys being stuck in traffic when they have somewhere to be, but we cannot always avoid bad traffic, especially during rush hour in Seoul. In this lesson, we introduce some useful expressions that you can use when you are stuck in or expecting bad traffic, as well as some other advanced expressions related to traffic.

1.

차가 막혀요.

= The traffic is bad.

* 막히다 = to be clogged, to be stuck, to be blocked

2.

차가 많이 막히네요.

= (I see that) the traffic is really bad.

* You can use this when you call someone to let them know you are going to be late.

3.

차가 너무 많이 막혀서 오늘은 차 두고 나왔어요.

= The traffic is really bad today, so I left my car at home.

* 두다 = to leave (something)

4.

지금은 차가 많이 막히는 시간이라서 지하철 타고 가는 게 빠를 거예요.

= Now is the time (of day) when traffic is bad, so it will be faster to take the subway.

* 시간이라서 and 시간이어서 have the same meaning. Both -(이)라서 and -아/어/여서 connect a reason with a result, but -(이)라서 can only be attached to -이다 and -이 아니다. -이라서 and -이 아니라서 are also used more often than -이어서 and -이 아니어서 in colloquial language.

Track 57

5.

차가 좀 막혀서 늦을 것 같아요.

= Traffic is bad, so I will be a bit late.

6.

차가 심하게 막혀서 20분 정도 늦을 것 같아요.

= Traffic is really bad, so I think I will be about 20 minutes late.

* 심하다 = severely, seriously

7.

보통 이 시간대에는 차가 안 막히는데, 오늘은 좀 많이 막히네요.

= Traffic is usually not bad at this time of day, but today it is pretty bad.

8.

어제 여기 지나가는 데에 한 시간 걸렸어요.

= It took me one hour to pass through this place yesterday.

9.

서울에서는 출퇴근 시간에 운전하면 차 막히는 거 각오해야 돼요.

= If you drive in Seoul around rush hour, you have to be ready for some bad traffic.

* 출퇴근 시간 = rush hour

** 각오하다 = to be mentally ready

10.

차만 안 막히면 10분 안에 갈 수 있는 거리예요.

= If traffic is not bad, it takes about 10 minutes to get there.

11.

이쪽 길은 많이 막히는 것 같으니까 다른 길로 갈게요.

= It looks like traffic is very bad on this road, so I will take another route.

12.

거기 지금쯤 많이 막히지 않을까요?

= Don't you think the traffic there must be bad by now?

13.

차가 하나도 안 막혀서 빨리 왔어요.

= There was no traffic at all, so I got here fast.

Sample Dialogue

석진: 오늘 차가 많이 막히네요.

현우: 서울에서는 출퇴근 시간에 운전하면 차 막히는 거 각오해야 돼요.

석진: 아무리 그래도 이건 좀 심한 것 같아요. 차만 안 막히면 10분 안에 갈 수 있는 거리잖아요.

현우: 저 어제도 여기 지나가는 데에 한 시간 걸렸어요.

Seokjin: The traffic is bad today.

Hyunwoo: In Seoul, if you drive during rush hour, you should be prepared to get stuck in traffic.

Seokjin: No matter how true that is, I think this is really bad. You know that it only takes 10 minutes if traffic is not bad.

Hyunwoo: It took me an hour to pass through here yesterday, too.

199

✏ Exercises for Lesson *29*

Fill in the blanks to match the English translation.

Check the answers on **p. 219**

1. 차만 안 막히면 10분 안에 갈 수 있는 ( ).

= If traffic is not bad, it takes about 10 minutes.

2. 차가 막혀서 좀 ( ).

= Traffic is bad, so I will be a bit late.

3. 어제 여기 지나가는 데에 ( ).

= It took me one hour to pass through this place yesterday.

4. 이쪽 길은 많이 막히는 것 같으니까 ( ).

= It looks like the traffic is very bad on this road, so I will take another route.

5. 차가 너무 많이 막혀서 오늘은 차 ( ) 나왔어요.

= The traffic is really bad today, so I left my car at home.

200

LESSON **30**

Sentence Building Drill 17

Sentence Building Drill 17

In this series, we focus on how you can use the grammatical rules and expressions that you have learned previously to train yourself to comfortably make Korean sentences.

Track 59

We will start off with THREE key sentences and practice changing different parts of these sentences so that you do not end up simply memorizing the same three sentences. We want you to be able to make your own Korean sentences as flexibly and confidently as possible.

Key Sentence (1)
이렇게 제출할 바에는, 제출 안 해서 후회하는 한이 있더라도 그냥 제출 안 하겠어요.
= If I have to submit it like this, I would just not turn it in, even if that means I will regret it because I didn't turn it in.

Key Sentence (2)
어제 경화 씨가 밖에 나가더니 강아지를 데리고 오더라고요.
= Kyung-hwa went outside yesterday and then came back with a puppy.

Key Sentence (3)

어제 공연이 끝나기가 무섭게 사람들이 다 나갔다면서요.

= As soon as the performance was over yesterday, I heard that everyone went outside.

Expansion & Variation Practice with Key Sentence (1)

0. Original Sentence:

이렇게 제출할 바에는, 제출 안 해서 후회하는 한이 있더라도 그냥 제출 안 하겠어요.

= If I have to submit it like this, I would just not turn it in, even if that means I will regret it

because I didn't turn it in.

Track
59

1.

이렇게 제출할 바에는

= If I have to submit it like this, (I would rather)...

처음부터 다시 할 바에는

= If I have to do it again from the beginning, (I would rather)...

경화 씨랑 같이 앉을 바에는

= If I have to sit with Kyung-hwa, (I would rather)...

혼자서 영화를 볼 바에는

= If I have to watch a movie by myself, (I would rather)...

사람들 앞에서 창피를 당할 바에는

= If I have to embarrass myself in front of people, (I would rather)...

2.

제출 안 해서 후회하는 한이 있더라도 그냥 제출 안 하겠어요.

= Even if I end up regretting it because I didn't turn it in, I would just not turn it in.

전체 내용을 다 바꾸는 한이 있더라도 괜찮아요.

= Even if I end up changing all the content, it is okay.

내일 다시 오는 한이 있더라도, 오늘은 여기까지만 할 거예요.

= Even if I end up having to come back tomorrow, I will stop working on it now.

늦게 자는 한이 있더라도, 이 책 다 읽을 거예요.

= Even if I end up going to bed late, I will finish this book.

밤을 새우는 한이 있더라도 이거 오늘 다 끝내세요.

= Even if you end up staying up all night, finish this today.

Expansion & Variation Practice with Key Sentence (2)

0. Original Sentence:

어제 경화 씨가 밖에 나가더니 강아지를 데리고 오더라고요.

= Kyung-hwa went outside yesterday and then came back with a puppy.

Track
59

1.

어제 경화 씨가 밖에 나가더니

= Kyung-hwa went outside yesterday and then...

아침부터 눈이 많이 오더니

= It was snowing a lot starting from morning and then...

석진 씨가 어제 커피를 많이 마시더니

= Seokjin was drinking a lot of coffee yesterday and now...

예지 씨가 운동을 열심히 하더니

= Yeji worked out hard and now...

스테파니 씨가 한국어를 매일 공부하더니

= Stephanie studied Korean every day and now...

2.

강아지를 데리고 오더라고요.

= (I saw that) she brought a puppy.

잠이 안 오더라고요.

= I could not sleep.

* "잠이 안 왔어요" is the plain past tense, but "잠이 안 오더라고요" shows that you are giving an explanation for why you are tired.

이 영화 생각보다 재미있더라고요.

= I found this movie to be more interesting than I expected.

거기는 항상 사람이 많더라고요.

= (I found that) that place is always crowded.

* This implies that you are talking about a place you have seen or have been to.

저는 이 옷이 제일 편하더라고요.

= (I find that) these clothes are the most comfortable.

Track 59

Expansion & Variation Practice with Key Sentence (3)

0. Original Sentence:

어제 공연이 끝나기가 무섭게 사람들이 다 나갔다면서요.

= As soon as the performance was over yesterday, I heard that everybody went outside.

* Please note that -기가 무섭게 has nothing to do with being scared, but rather means "as soon as". It has a slightly stronger meaning than -자마자 which also means "as soon as".

1.

어제 공연이 끝나기가 무섭게 = As soon as the performance was over yesterday...

비가 그치기가 무섭게 = As soon as the rain stopped...

전화벨이 울리기가 무섭게 = As soon as the phone rang...

말이 끝나기가 무섭게 = As soon as I finished talking...

문이 열리기가 무섭게 = As soon as the door opened...

2.

사람들이 다 나갔다면서요. = I heard that everybody went outside.

어제 다혜 씨 만났다면서요. = I heard that you met Dahye yesterday.

아무도 안 왔다면서요. = I heard that nobody came.

교통사고가 있었다면서요. = I heard that there was a traffic accident.

시험에 합격했다면서요. = I heard that you passed the exam.

Track 59

Sample Dialogue

Track
60

석진: 경화 씨, 그 마술 쇼 티켓 벌써
　　　매진됐다면서요?

경화: 네, 판매 시작하기가 무섭게 다
　　　팔렸다더라고요. 너무 가고 싶었는데...

석진: 그 마술사 인기가 대단하다더니
　　　정말이네요.

경화: 다음에는 제일 비싼 자리를 예매하는
　　　한이 있더라도 꼭 갈 거예요.

*Seokjin: Kyung-hwa, I heard that tickets for that
magic show are sold out.*

*Kyung-hwa: Yes. I found out that they sold out as
soon as they went on sale. I really wanted
to go...*

*Seokjin: People say that that magician is really
popular, and it is true!*

*Kyung-hwa: I'll definitely go next time even if I
have to reserve the most expensive seat.*

Check the answers on **p. 219**

Write the phrase that can fill in the two blanks.

1.

처음부터 다시 할 ....

= If I have to do it again from the beginning, (I would rather)...

경화 씨랑 같이 앉을 ....

= If I have to sit with Kyung-hwa, (I would rather)...

Answer: ( )

2.

말이 ....

= As soon as I finished talking...

어제 공연이 ....

= As soon as the performance was over yesterday...

Answer: ( )

3.

늦게 자는 ...., 이 책 다 읽을 거예요.

= Even if I end up going to bed late, I will finish this book.

밤을 새는 .... 이거 오늘 다 끝내세요.

= Even if you end up staying up all night, finish this today.

Answer: ( )

✏ *Exercises for Lesson* **30**

4.

강아지를 데리고 오 ....

= (I saw that) she brought a puppy.

거기는 항상 사람이 많........................... .

= (I found that) that place is always crowded.

Answer: (   )

5.

예지 씨가 운동을 열심히 하...........................

= Yeji worked out hard and now...

아침부터 눈이 많이 오...........................

= It was snowing a lot starting from morning and then...

Answer: (   )

Jeju Mackerel
(제주도 고등어)

Jeju Island is the largest island in South Korea. It has been dubbed the Hawaii of Korea and is home to an abundance of wind and rocks. It is known for its strong women that helped bring in wealth to the island while the men did not work. The wind in Jeju is strong and is even more powerful when it rains. If you want to stay somewhat dry in Jeju during the rainy season, turn in your umbrella for a poncho. Due to the wind, the rain almost seems like it is falling horizontally rather than vertically. Jeju is an island made by volcanoes and because of this you will find basalt, black porous rocks, all around the island. But these are not the only things you can find in Jeju. If you are someone who likes to try new food from different places, Jeju has quite a bit to offer.

One of my favorite things to eat in Jeju is mackerel (고등어). This fish can be found quite easily here in Jeju and many restaurants offer up different ways to eat it. My very first introduction to mackerel was actually on my first trip to Jeju. I went with some friends to a restaurant that overlooked a harbor on the oceanfront. Small boats were docked and swaying a bit from the ocean's waves. We walked into the restaurant and sat down and I let my friends do the ordering.

This particular restaurant served raw mackerel. I love raw fish so I was really excited to try mackerel raw. Once we got our meal, we were told there is a certain way to eat it. If you are familiar with raw fish, you might know about dipping it in soy sauce or wrapping it in lettuce with a bit of ssamjang (쌈장), a kind of pepper paste. But with mackerel, it is a bit different.

First, you get a strip of seaweed and place some rice on it. Then, add some chives (부추). Now that you have the base for your bite, you can either dip the mackerel in soy sauce and place it on top of everything or you can add some ssamjang. Either way is delicious. Then, simply eat it. And since you are in Jeju eating some of the freshest mackerel around, you might as well wash it down with Halla Mountain soju. This soju is made in Jeju and goes down quite smoothly. If you really want to impress your Korean friends, ask for a bottle at room temperature. This is how the people of Jeju typically drink Halla Mountain soju.

Now, eating mackerel raw is not the only way to eat it. Understandably, some may not enjoy eating raw fish, but do not let that stop you from trying this delicious fish in other ways. Another way you can try it is by having a mackerel sandwich. It might sound a bit odd at first, but trust me on this, it is absolutely delicious. Everyone I have ever recommended this place to has loved it. It is a nice cosy restaurant in Seogwipo City called Sol Fish. It is located near the famous Lee Jeong-Seop Street Culture Street. If you are in the area, check out this restaurant and try a bite of their mackerel sandwich. The owner is also quite nice and you will not be forgetting your mackerel sandwich experience anytime soon.

If you are feeling a bit more daring, there is yet another way to try mackerel. You can fish for it! If you are prone to seasickness, they do offer drinks to help with this so you can still enjoy the trip without worrying about getting sick. Once you are out in the boat, they will give you a rod with some hooks on it to catch your own fish. There are various types of fish you can catch but we caught quite a bit of mackerel on our trip. One of the cool things about fishing is that on some of the boats they will serve you some of the raw fish from your catch right there on the spot. Other boats offer a stove to cook it up. Then, once you get back to shore, you can go to one of the nearby restaurants where they will cook the rest of your catch for you. We had some of it raw and had the rest battered and fried. Boy! It was one of the most delicious meals I have ever had. The fish was as fresh as it could be and since we were the ones who caught it, it was that much more satisfying.

As you can see, these are just a few of the many ways you can eat mackerel. Other places make a mackerel stew, which they say is a great way to cure a hangover. Whether it cures hangovers or not, trying mackerel in Jeju is a must. And if you do try this amazing food, tell us about it. We would love to hear about your experience with Jeju Island's famous fish.

Written by Johnny Bland

Level 9을 모두 끝냈어요*!*
정말 축하합니다*!!*

ANSWERS

for Level 9, Lessons 1 ~ 30

Answers for Level 9, Lesson 1

1. 손을 놓다

2. 손을 씻다

3. 손이 크다

4. 손에 땀을 쥐다

5. 손에 익다

Answers for Level 9, Lesson 2

1. 사 버렸어요.

2. 떨어져 버렸어요.

3. 벌써 다 말해 버렸어요.

4. 컴퓨터가 멈춰 버렸어요.

5. 영화가 벌써 시작해 버렸어요.

Answers for Level 9, Lesson 3

1. ①

2. ③

3. ②

4. ④

5. ③

Answers for Level 9, Lesson 4

1. 감기에 걸리고 말았어요.

2. 이곳도 사막이 되고 말았어요.

3. 너무 어두워서 머리를 벽에 부딪히고 말았어요.

4. 범인을 쫓아갔지만 놓치고 말았어요.

5. 가겠다는 약속을 하고 말았어요.

Answers for Level 9, Lesson 5

1. 불안해요.

2. 경화 씨가 늦으면 어떡하죠?

3. (문제가) 잘 해결됐으면 좋겠어요.

4. 마음이 안 놓여요.

5. 걱정돼 죽겠어요.

Answers for Level 9, Lesson 6

1. 발을 끊다

2. 발 디딜 틈이 없다

3. 한발 늦다

4. 발이 넓다

5. 발 벗고 나서다

Answers for Level 9, Lesson 7

1. 비 (非)

2. 비공식 (非公式)

3. 비상구 (非常口)

4. 비회원 (非會員)

5. 비공개 (非公開)

Answers for Level 9, Lesson 8

1. 죄송한데요, 혹시 전화기 좀 빌릴 수 있을까요?

2. 저 잠깐만 도와주실 수 있나요?

3. 편의점에 가는 김에 물 좀 사다 줄 수 있어요?

4. 돌아오는 길에 우유 좀 사다 줄 수 있어요?

5. 어제 제가 부탁한 거 잊지 마세요.

Answers for Level 9, Lesson 9

1. 웃음

2. 울음

3. 믿음

4. 앎

5. 삶

6. 춤

7. 잠

8. 젊음

9. 꿈

10. 졸음

Answers for Level 9, Lesson 10

1. 주연 씨가 사람들한테 말해 버렸어요.

2. 사고 말았어요.

3. 임

4. 음

5. 함

Answers for Level 9, Lesson 11

1. 마음이 놓이다

2. 마음이 통하다

3. 마음에 걸리다

4. 마음에 없는 말을 하다

5. 마음을 먹다

Answers for Level 9, Lesson 12

1. 피곤해 보여요.

2. 이거 매워 보여요.

3. 이 영화는 재미없어 보여요.

4. 사장님 기분이 안 좋아 보여요.

5. 이 케이크가 맛있어 보여서 샀는데, 너무 달아요.

Answers for Level 9, Lesson 13

1. 신 (新)

2. 신혼 (新婚)

3. 신입생 (新入生)

4. 신기록 (新記錄)

5. 신세대 (新世代)

Answers for Level 9, Lesson 14

1. 막심해요

2. 말걸

3. 괜히

4. 좋았을 텐데요

5. 나을 뻔했어요

6. 싶어요

Answers for Level 9, Lesson 15

1. 기분이 상하다

2. 기분을 풀다

3. 기분 전환을 하다

4. 기분 내키는 대로

5. 기분이 들뜨다

Answers for Level 9, Lesson 16

1. 제가 점심 살 테니까

2. 저는 먼저 갈 테니까

3. 나머지는 제가 할 테니까

4. 저는 뛰어갈 테니까

5. 아직 뜨거울 테니까

Answers for Level 9, Lesson 17

1. 한번 시작한 이상 or 일단 시작한 이상

2. 여기까지 온 이상

3. 아주 아프지 않은 이상 or 많이 아프지 않은 이상 or 심하게 아프지 않은 이상

4. 이 방에 들어온 이상

5. 가족이 아닌 이상

Answers for Level 9, Lesson 18

1. 나중에 후회할까 봐

2. 차가 막힐까 봐

3. 아이가 실망할까 봐

4. 배고프실까 봐

5. 이 책 필요하실까 봐

Answers for Level 9, Lesson 19

1. 얼마 만

2. 지내요

3. 보는 거죠

4. 오랜만

5. 보고

Answers for Level 9, Lesson 20

1. 한국까지 온 이상 (한국까지 왔으니까 is also possible.)

2. 혼자 하면 힘들 테니(까) (혼자 하면 힘들 거니까 is also possible.)

3. 혼자서도 할 수 있다니까요.

4. 사실은 아주 건강한 편이에요. ("사실은 꽤 건강한 편이에요" is also possible.)

5. 지금 가면 차가 막힐 테니(까) 나중에 가세요.

Answers for Level 9, Lesson 21

1. 생각이 나다

2. 생각이 없다

3. 생각이 간절하다

4. 생각하기도 싫다

5. 생각에 잠기다

Answers for Level 9, Lesson 22

1. 示 means "to show", and 視 means "to see".

2. 시각 (視覺)

3. 시력 (視力)

4. 시선 (視線)

5. 예시 (例示)

6. 예시 (例示) = example, illustration

Answers for Level 9, Lesson 23

1. 저는 샤워하면서 노래를 불러요.

2. 저는 잠을 자면서 많이 움직여요.

3. 저는 학교에 다니면서 아르바이트를 많이 했어요.

4. 알지도 못하면서 쉽게 말하지 마세요.

5. 그 사람은 제 친구(이)면서 동시에 선생님이에요.

Answers for Level 9, Lesson 24

1. 다음 달에 이사 간다면서요?

2. 벌써 다 끝났다면서요?

3. 아직 학생이라면서요!

4. 잘 모르는 사이라면서요!

5. 형이 의사라면서요?

Answers for Level 9, Lesson 25

1. 길 좀 물을

2. 어느 쪽

3. 아세요

4. 잘 모르겠네요 (잘 모르겠어요 or 잘 모르겠는데요 is also possible)

5. 이쪽으로

Answers for Level 9, Lesson 26

1. 시간이 남아돌다

2. 시간을 내다

3. 시간을 되돌리다

4. 시간을 할애하다

5. 한국 시간으로

Answers for Level 9, Lesson 27

1. A

2. B

3. B

4. A

5. A

Answers for Level 9, Lesson 28

1. 있겠어요

2. 어차피 or 이왕

3. 낫겠어요 or 나을 거예요

4. 차라리

5. 바에는 or 바에야 or 바에

Answers for Level 9, Lesson 29

1. 거리예요

2. 늦을 것 같아요 or 늦을 거예요

3. 한 시간 걸렸어요

4. 다른 길로 갈게요

5. 두고 or 놓고

Answers for Level 9, Lesson 30

1. 바에는 or 바에야 or 바에

2. 끝나기가 무섭게 or 끝나기가 바쁘게 or 끝나자마자

3. 한이 있더라도

4. 더라고요

5. 더니

Notes On Using This Book

Colored Text

Colored text indicates that there is an accompanying audio file. You can download the MP3 audio files at **talktomeinkorean.com/audio**.

Hyphen

Some grammar points have a hyphen attached at the beginning, such as -이/가, -(으)ㄹ 거예요, -(으)려고 하다, and -은/는커녕. This means that the grammar point is dependent, so it needs to be attached to another word such as a noun, a verb, or a particle.

Parentheses

When a grammar point includes parentheses, such as -(으)ㄹ 거예요 or (이)랑, this means that the part in the parentheses can be omitted depending on the word it is attached to.

Slash

When a grammar point has a slash, such as -아/어/여서 or -은/는커녕, this means that only one of the syllables before or after the slash can be used at a time. In other words, -은/는커녕 is used as either -은커녕 or -는커녕, depending on the word it is attached to.

Descriptive Verb

In TTMIK lessons, adjectives in English are referred to as "descriptive verbs" because they can be conjugated as verbs depending on the tense.